Ignite the Fire

Kindling

a Passion

for Christ

in Your Kids

BARRY & CAROL ST. CLAIR

Chariot Victor Publishing
A Division of Cook Communications

Chariot Victor Publishing
A division of Cook Communications, Colorado Springs, Colorado 80918
Cook Communications, Paris, Ontario, Canada
Kingsway Communications, Eastbourne, England

**Published in association with the literary agency of Alive Communications,
1465 Kelly Johnson Blvd., Suite 320, Colorado Springs, CO 80920.**

Cover and Interior Design: Image Studios

1 2 3 4 5 6 7 8 9 10 Printing/Year 03 02 01 00 99

Library of Congress Cataloging-in-Publication Data

St. Clair, Barry.
    Ignite the fire/by Barry and Carol St. Clair.
        p.   cm.
    Includes bibliographical references.
    ISBN   1-56476-747-7
    1. Parenting—Religious aspects—Christianity.
    2. Christian education of children.
    I. St. Clair, Carol.   II. Title.
    BV4529.8'45—dc21   98-53689
                                                        CIP

Contents

With Gratitude

Thanks to all of the people who have helped make this book possible. No one writes a book without serious input and significant support. Appreciation goes to Susan Nichols and the rest of the Reach Out staff team for covering my responsibilities while I wrote. Sharon Stanton spent hours doing final edits. Karl Schaller, thanks for navigating some difficult issues with grace and dignity. Greg Clouse, your patience kept the pressure off when the deadline kept having to be pushed back due to the circumstances. Scott, Cameron, Katie, Bart, Jonathan, and Ginny, you stuck with this project at the toughest time in your life. I'm blessed to have you for my children.

Dedication

Buddy and Bev Price, Carol's parents

Howard and Kitty St. Clair, Barry's parents

The fire that burned brightly in you has now spread over two generations. Your prayers, love, and encouragement kept the flame burning in us.

Melinda Dellas
Wanda McSwain
Ginger Miller
Edwina Morgan
Kitti Murray
Julie Norton
Katie Purcell
Regina Walters
Regina Williams

Thanks for taking one day a week the last few months of Carol's life to fast and pray for her and serve our family on the day of your fast.

A Most Painful Book to Write

Writing this book has been one of the most difficult and painful experiences of my life.

Carol and I sat on the floor in the corner of a bookstore surrounded by 150 books on parenting. We questioned seriously why another book could possibly be needed on this subject. After thinking about it for several days we concluded that we would write this book, not because another book on parenting is needed, but because we wanted to encourage other parents by letting them look into the window of our family. We felt that our intimate relationship with God, our love for each other, and the unique ways the Lord had worked in the lives of our children would make it worth the effort to write the book.

Over hot tea we excitedly outlined the book in the fall. We loved coming up with the stories about our kids that we put in the book. After five of these "outline days" we were ready to write. We planned to have half of the book written by year end.

Then the first blow struck. Carol had cancer. We told each other that after she recovered from the surgery we would work on the book in January. She recovered.

Then the second blow struck us when we realized that she needed follow-up treatment. That turned into seven hard weeks of therapy that took us through March. During that time we talked through chapters, then I would write, knowing that in April we would get on track together to finish the book. We put cancer behind us with a family trip to the beach for spring break. My, did we have fun! All of us walked and ran on the beach. Carol was right in there with us.

But then the third blow struck us. By the end of the week at the beach she could hardly get out of her chair. We thought she had overdone it on the exercise. But after seeing a round of doctors when we got home, we discovered that she had scleroderma, an autoimmune disease. While we tried to figure out what this meant, I kept on consulting with Carol and writing. Carol kept on advising me and planning our Katie's wedding. On June 20th, Katie got married. Carol was ill, but she looked gorgeous.

Then the final blow struck. What normally takes fifteen years to do, scleroderma did to her in four months. Trying to fight it was like shooting a squirt gun at a forest fire. On August 2nd, Carol died. The heart of our family was ripped out. The pain has been severe!

One of the most difficult things I have ever done is to pick up two chapters of this book that were yet unwritten, and write them. One reason for the difficulty was that those two chapters were the heart and soul of Carol's parenting philosophy. We put off writing them, thinking that she would get well enough to write them herself. She never did. So about three weeks after Carol died, I sat down with notes from talks she had given, with illustrations scribbled in the margins, and wrote those two chapters as if she were still with us. It was a terribly bitter and wonderfully sweet experience, at the same time. While writing I was reminded again and again what an incredible wife and mom she had been. She embodied the principles of this book.

From this experience I draw two conclusions:

1. Out of the pain of Carol's death, the loss of our wife and mother, I want you to know that our family identifies with you in whatever pain you are facing.

2. Carol's absence has made our family look back and see that all that really matters when death comes is Jesus, family, friends, and heaven. Looking through that rearview mirror makes kindling a passion for Christ in our kids all the more significant. My prayer is that you will see the high value of that *now* and pursue it with every fiber of your being.

—*Barry St. Clair*

Fiery Words from Passionate Kids

BACK ROW: Barry, Katie, Carol, Jonathan, Ginny, Bart
FRONT ROW: Scott, Cameron

When the Lord ignites a fire in someone's heart, then the fire spreads to others.

We, the St. Clair kids, saw the fire of Christ in our parents. When they talked to us about what attracted them to one another, a passion for Christ was at the top of the list. Because of their love for us, that passion has been both attractive to us and contagious. God has used them to ignite the fire of Christ in each one of us.

Scott
Growing up in a home with two parents committed to living for Christ, I was continually exposed to church services, family devotional, prayer meetings, Bible studies, and the like. However, as I

reflect on the impact my parents had on my spiritual journey, their living examples, more than any words or activities, made the deepest impression on me.

Mom and Dad each modeled Christ in their own unique ways. While many thoughts come to mind of my dad, one constant memory has challenged me the most. During high school, I woke up every morning at 6 A.M. And every day, I saw the light on in my Dad's study outside my room, knowing that he was starting his day by spending time with God in prayer and Bible study. This daily act revealed his deep desire to follow Christ, and it challenged me to develop that same passion for knowing God.

My mom's life was one characterized by sacrifice. Her sacrificial love started with her family and spread outward to involve countless other people. She truly "considered others better than herself," giving up many of her own needs and pursuits to serve others. Instead of one standout memory of Mom, my mind is flooded with images I see of her reaching out to meet the needs of others. Even during the last year of her life (1998), as she courageously and vigorously battled disease, she maintained a humble heart of service. Mom lived out—very practically—how to love God by laying down her life for other people.

Cameron (Scott's wife)
Over the past several years, my in-laws have given me many gifts—some tangible and others intangible. Carol, my mother-in-law, gave me the gifts of love and total acceptance, making me feel as if I were her own child. She gave these gifts through exam and holiday care packages while I was in college, encouraging phone calls the night before big tests or presentations, and listening ears when we were able to spend time together. Barry, my father-in-law, has given me the gift of wise counsel on topics ranging from marriage, to freedom in Christ, to how to concoct a healthy fruit shake! Because of Barry and Carol's generosity in sharing their gifts, my joining the St. Clair family has been one of the biggest blessings in my life.

Interestingly, however, Barry and Carol gave me the greatest *gift they could possibly give me years before I met their son: they ignited within Scott a desire to follow Jesus. Before Scott was born, Barry and Carol chose 1 Timothy 6:11 as his life verse: "But you, man of God, flee from all this, and pursue righteousness, godliness, faith, love, endurance and gentleness." As a child, Scott watched his parents pursue righteousness and godliness as they spent time in God's Word and in His church. He saw Barry and Carol strive for faith and endurance in the face of trials, big and small, as they clung to God's promises. Scott knew that his parents, like God, loved him unconditionally, and he knew that his mom's gentle back-scratches and his dad's goodnight kisses reflected something of the Father's gentleness. After Scott accepted Jesus Christ as his own Savior, his parents taught him, by word and through example, how to grow in his faith. By God's grace through Barry and Carol, Scott is a man of God who seeks the "fruits" of 1 Timothy 6:11.*

The greatest gift Barry and Carol have given me is a godly husband. Because they pointed Scott toward Jesus, "future generations will be told about the Lord. They will proclaim his righteousness to a people yet unborn" (Ps. 22:30b-31).

Katie

Not until college did I clearly recognize what makes our family unique, what sets me apart. The common component in the lives of my parents (as well as my extended family of grandparents, aunts, uncles, cousins) is a deep, genuine understanding of the love of God displayed in His Son—Jesus Christ.

Many of my friends come from Christian homes, yet few of them have been "discipled" by their parents. Daddy and Mommy sacrificed twenty-plus years of their energy and dreams to demonstrate the life of Christ to me. This book will illustrate the countless examples of their patience, creativity, mistakes, and efforts. If I could describe the way my parents displayed a passion for Jesus (beyond leading me to the knowledge of this grace) it would be found in the "little things" of everyday. My parents lived like Christ in a RADICAL way each day before my very eyes. The Bible was our source of knowledge and strength. We memorized verses as children. We read stories from it every night. We sang praise songs on car trips. We openly shared our hearts. We prayed together as a family. We went overseas on missions trips. We were disciplined for disobedience because God disciplines those He loves. The life of Christ was lived out daily in practical ways to us as children, adolescents, and adults. By catching a glimpse of their passion for our Savior, my life will never be the same.

Bart Garrett (Katie's husband)

From my first contact with the St. Clairs my freshman year in college I knew there was something very different about their family. I have been around many Christian families but still had not experienced the unique God-centered atmosphere I always associated with being around the St. Clairs. I soon began to understand that the family was constantly and consistently joined in prayer. Whether it was around the dinner table, at bedtime, or stealing a few brief moments at the front door before the start of a day, the family experienced a grace and richness and closeness that could only come from the Lord through prayer. This prayer was never forced or uncomfortable because it was a natural outpouring from a mom and a dad that loved their children, but more importantly, loved their God with all their heart, soul, mind, and strength. A family cannot help but become bonded in love for one another if they are together, hand-in-hand, entering the throne room of the Lord each day and experiencing the mercy, grace, and peace that He so freely gives to His children.

Jonathan

When I was six years old, Dad led me in the sinner's prayer of repentance, and I asked Jesus into my heart. Mom tucked me in bed every night of my life until I moved to college. My parents prayed with me and for me every day. I would open up my lunch to find an encouraging note. I would come home from school to find my room in order with an uplifting verse on my bed. They disciplined me in love, and they cried with me through the pain and failures of my life. They took me on special trips, accompanied me to church, and always encouraged me to pursue Christ with more passion.

However, apart from my salvation, none of these acts of love would have impacted my life for Jesus had they not already abandoned themselves to God. Their determined purpose, long before I came on the scene, was to know Jesus Christ. When I woke up early in the morning to spend time with God (as Dad taught me to do when he discipled me), Dad was already in his study doing the same. When I came home from school in the afternoon, Mom's Bible was open on the dinner table, along with her journal, prayer lists, and Scripture memory box. My parents, imperfect as they were, not only modeled Christ and nurtured me in a moral, loving Christian home, they themselves also pursued Jesus Christ with undying passion, which became the life-giving, grace-abounding, transforming power of our family.

Ginny
When I was born, my brothers and sisters were fourteen, eleven, and eight. Growing up, I really had five parents! Everybody loved me, but everybody told me what to do. My dad helped Jonathan accept Christ. One night when my parents were on a date, Jonathan helped me accept Christ.

My parents took me to church, read the Bible with me, and prayed with me, along with a whole lot of other things.

My whole family has surrounded me with love and their love has led me to love Jesus more!

All of us agree, our parents definitely were not perfect. But we have been deeply impacted by their love for Christ, each other, and us. We hope to pass that same legacy along to our children in the next generation.

Thanks, Mom and Dad!

By Sheer Grace

Every family is different. Each child is unique. Stating those two realities makes it clear that this book is not the last word on raising children. Nor is this book a research project. It comes to you through the lens of one family's experience. Because of that we can state with certainy that this is not the only way to raise children who have a passion for God. Even though the Action Principles that drive this book are biblical, they will be applied in a radically different manner by each person who reads the book—with radically different results.

Up front we want to confess to you, our readers, that when people ask us how we raised our kids to love God, we have only one response: "By the sheer grace of God!" We recognize that we have been blessed with a family that has responded well to these principles and because of that we had the confidence to write the book. At the same time we want to make it very clear that we recognize that "the way we did it" is not the last word on raising children, and certainly not the only way.

Truthfully, we know people who have applied these principles as well or better than we have, and they have not been blessed with the same results. God, in His grace and sovereignty, is working each situation out differently. If you are in a situation where your children are not responding, we want this book to become a solid shot of encouragement to keep you dreaming for your children. Hang in there and continue to trust that God will accomplish His unique purpose for your child.

We want to offer hope and help to parents who have not seen positive results and who thus may be. That may have caused you to seriously questioning their parenting abilities. At times all of us feel like we fall into one of these three "black holes of parenting":

1. *The "Done It's."* Some parents will feel like they already know these principles and have acted on them, yet the results have been far from perfect. You are dealing with a consistently rebellious and wayward child.

2. *The "Haven't Done It's."* Others will read the chapters, recognize the truth of the advice, and quickly admit they have not been taking the kind of action they need to take. You may feel like it is too late. Or you may compare yourself to other parents or (God forbid) to us, and feel like you fall far short of the ideal parent.

3. *The "Half Has Done It's."* Still others come from a single-parent home, or a home where the other spouse is not going in the same direction. Having watched many situations like these, we stand amazed continually at how well you do.

In light of this we want to keep in mind that beyond what we do as parents, two very significant factors are constantly at work in the parenting process.

1. *Our children's role.* Parents can do everything perfectly to create the right environment, but at some point what happens depends solely on how that child responds to the Lord. If that rebellious child is a believer, then he will stand before Christ one day and have to give an account of his life. We, as parents, can say, "We need to do all that we can, but there is a limit to our responsibility." We cannot force our child to do anything, really. If a child chooses to reject our faith and us, what can we do at that point but pray?

2. *God's role.* We have watched parents do everything to create the wrong environment and yet their children grow up to love God totally. Frankly, we do not understand that. But God does. We have watched parents put together a positive environment and their children walk out the door. But like the Prodigal Son, God has a plan for your child. Rebellious children who return to the Lord often have an intensity about Jesus that others don't have because they have been "The Prodigal Son." God calls us to pray faithfully. When we do, He will act on our behalf. We know hundreds of children who

have come back to God as the result of God hearing the prayers of a praying parent. Don't give up.

Our prayer for each and all of us is that:

• We will feel free to use the Action Points but not to feel guilty if they do not get perfect results.

• We will have hope that each setback will be temporary and that ultimately God will get us to our goal of raising our children to be passionate about Jesus. To get there, we will probably experience some unexpected twists and turns.

• We will allow God time to complete His work. We care so deeply for our children that we want immediate results. When those results don't come, we beat up on ourselves with a string of feelings: bitterness, guilt, fear, anger. We do not need to give up hope, especially when our children are pushing us away.

• We will improve our prayer lives as we run to God with our feelings of total inadequacy, and as we look to God to do His divine work in our children's lives.

When all is said and done, our prayer is that you will hang on to this promise:

"He who fears the Lord has a secure fortress, and for his children it will be a refuge" (Prov. 14:26).

Set the Pace

**How do we set an example
that creates a passion for Christ in our children?**

PARENTS AREN'T PERFECT. They never have been. They never will be.

A young couple, missionaries to the Philippines, wanted to visit us. They had started their family, felt inadequate to raise their children, and wanted to talk to a family who had successfully traveled down the parenting road. We agreed to talk. After dinner, they peppered us with questions about raising children. Jonathan, about ten at the time, acted up at dinner. We sent him to his room. A few moments later I stepped out to check on Jonathan. His room was located next to the den, where we were talking. He had locked the door. I asked him to open it. He refused. In a louder voice I asked him to open the door. Again he refused, but this time he yelled his refusal, certainly within earshot of our guests. I interrupted Carol's conversation with our guests to tell her I needed her help. Both of us went to Jonathan's room and insisted that he open the door. He yelled his refusal even louder this time.

Meanwhile, our parenting disciples sat in the den taking it all in. We decided to leave Jonathan alone, not so much for his good, but to stem the mounting tide of embarrassment. We sat down again with our guests, continuing the conversation and trying to cover for Jonathan's behavior. A few minutes later I thought it best to check on Jonathan again. This time I received no response when I knocked on his locked door. I yelled louder and louder, hoping our guests were deaf. When it became clear that he was not going to answer, I went outside to his window. It was open, and he had disappeared. Jonathan had run away from home! Our unimpressed couple tried to help us track him down. We got into the car and finally found him a few blocks away. Spotting us, he ran harder and faster to evade us. We finally captured the boy. And we never heard from the missionary couple again.

Parents aren't perfect! Our "True Confessions" story makes that clear. We fit that imperfect category. After we spoke to Jonathan, we resolved the problem. On vacation this year we retold infamous childhood stories and rolled with laughter as Jonathan recounted the story about his "tyrannical oppressors." [*Note*: This is Jonathan's rendition of the story and has his approval for use here.]

"There Are Little Eyes upon You"
Despite our imperfections we are called to be parents. From God's perspective, that call goes much deeper than raising "good kids." Thousands of ideas, suggestions, pointers, and principles come at us about how to raise our children. Beyond

those, we must ignite a fire in our children that creates a passion to pursue God and His purposes. Our first action step: *Set the pace, model, create an example that provides our children with a very personal pattern to follow.*

At a Fellowship of Christian Athletes' camp in college I discovered this poem. Written for athletes, it nonetheless speaks powerfully to parents.

To Any Athlete
There are little eyes upon you,
And they're watching night and day;
There are little ears that quickly
Take in every word you say.
There are little hands all eager to do anything you do
And a little boy who's dreaming
Of the day he'll be like you.

You're the little fellow's idol;
You're the wisest of the wise,
In his little mind about you no suspicions ever rise;
He believes in you devoutly
Holds that all you say and do,
He will say and do, in your way
When he's a grown-up like you.

There's a wide-eyed little fellow,
Who believes you're always right
And his ears are always open,
And he watches day and night;
You are setting an example
Every day in all you do,
For the little boy who's waiting
To grow up to be like you.

(Author unknown)

Our feelings of inadequacy about setting the right example for our children often overshadow the inspired truth of that poem. "My spouse is not perfect. I'm worse. Our home is not the best. We have made many mistakes. How can I possibly be a good example to my children?" Good point! You can't. But God can! And that is the key to *taking action* on every chapter in this book.

> **Parenting boils down to what our kids see us being passionate about!**

Passionately pursuing Jesus is "more caught than taught," to use a well-worn phrase. What we model for our children in relationships, attitudes, priorities, and actions shapes our children's lives. More than merely mouthing the right words, parenting boils down to what our kids see us being passionate about. So, what stokes your fire? Is Jesus the one who lights up your life, or is it something else? As Bob Buford communicated so graphically in his book *Halftime,* each person has to decide what one thing to put in the "black box." What is it going to be? For our families to passionately pursue God and His purposes, JESUS CHRIST must go into the box.

Begin with the End in Mind

One leadership guru strongly suggests that any successful venture begin with the end in mind. We suggest following the lead of the Apostle Paul, who consistently began with the end in mind.

> For what is our hope, our joy, or the crown
> in which we will glory in the presence of our
> Lord Jesus when he comes? Is it not you?
> Indeed, you are our glory and joy. (1 Thes.
> 2:19-20)

When it's all said and done, what will be "the crown in which we will glory"? Our work, church, friendships, sports, fun, and travel pale in comparison to our children. As Paul said, "You are our glory and joy." Paul's disciples became his "glory and joy" because of his investment in their lives. He took responsibility for their growth in their relationship to Jesus Christ. Our children will become our "crown" because we invest heavily in their becoming passionate followers of Jesus. Let's begin with that end in mind.

Making Jesus Christ the center of our home has been the overriding factor in any success we have had with our children. One year on a personal retreat to reaffirm our family's direction, we walked down the beach talking about parenting our children. We agreed that our discretionary time would go toward helping our children and their friends become passionate followers of Christ. In spite of our inadequacies, we decided to personally disciple our children according to their unique needs.

That discipleship expresses itself in two ways. One is the *informal process.* Day in and day out our children watch our lives and "catch Christ" from us. The other is the *formal process.* That involves structured times of instruction that help our children move toward maturity in their relationship with Christ. In both of these we model by our example and set the pace for our children. We hope to pass along to you the principles that have guided us through our struggle to model and set the pace.

People ask, "What can I do to ensure that my children turn out right?" Really, that's the wrong question. The real question is: "What can I do to help my child follow Jesus?" The answer centers around one essential factor: investing in formal and informal discipling relationships. After observing teenagers for over thirty years, discipling is clearly the number one way to influence a child's life. (Let's acknowledge that the willingness and teachability of our children greatly affect this process. If your children are not ready for that, then wait until they are.) To show us how to do that, the Apostle Paul provided the basic principles in 2 Timothy 2:1-2:

> You then, my son, be strong in the grace that is in Christ Jesus. And the things you have heard me say in the presence of many witnesses entrust to reliable men who will also be qualified to teach others.

[**Discipling is the number one way to influence a child's life.**]

Grow in Grace

Create the right *environment* for healthy growth. Just as proper nutrition, exercise, and sleep affect the health of our bodies, creating a "grace environment" affects the spiritual health of relationships at home. Grace creates that right environment.

Set the right *example*. This presents our children with a vivid picture of how to live for Christ. Grace is the spiritual power that allows us to do that.

Environment and *example*–these are two sides of the same coin of God's creative grace in our homes. That's why Paul said to Timothy: "My son, be strong in the grace that is in Christ Jesus" (2 Tim. 2:1). Yet what makes us strong in grace?

When the Apostle Paul asked God to take away his thorn in the flesh, God said to him, "My grace is sufficient for you, for my power is made perfect in weakness" (2 Cor. 12:9).

For many of us our "thorn in the flesh" is our inability to parent our children correctly. Our monstrous mistake occurs when we think we can create that environment or set that example in our own strength—and we keep trying. We don't have it. We never have. And we never will. Until we grasp that, admit it, and give up trying, we will never fully experience God's grace. That's why the Bible says, "God opposes the proud but gives grace to the humble" (James 4:6; see also Prov. 3:34).

God Himself tells us: My grace is all you need. My power works best in your weakness. Therefore, we can admit our weakness and allow the power of Christ to work through us.

According to John 1:14-16, grace works like this:

- Jesus came "full of grace and truth."
- We receive the fullness of His grace when we receive Him.
- He gives us all the grace we need no matter how difficult the situation—"grace upon grace."

Because Jesus died on the cross to forgive our sins and was resurrected to release eternal life in us, we have Christ living in us. Like an overflowing cup, the Holy Spirit works in, around, and through us to give us the ability to live the way God wants us to live. He gives us the fruit of the Spirit to reflect the character of Christ to our children (Gal. 5:22-23). He provides the gifts of the Spirit that motivate us and help us meet our children's needs (Rom. 12:3-8; 1 Cor. 12:1-11). He grants us power to reflect Christ and communicate about Him to our children (Acts 1:8).

That's "everyday parenting grace." It's like having a credit card with unlimited spending privileges. (Sounds great!) When we enter our personal card, nothing is in the account.

["Everyday parenting grace" gives us the ability to raise our children with the power of God!]

But when we put in the grace card, we have an unlimited amount of God's supernatural resources to raise our children. Which card do you prefer?

In every situation every day we have to continually make the choice about which card we will use. When we use the "grace card," we no longer live under the specter of having to perform to perfection in order to raise our children correctly. Rather, we have freedom, power, and strength knowing that we have moved beyond doing everything right to letting God empower us to make right parenting decisions. Now our example doesn't depend on what we do, but on what God does through us. And over the years our children will see the Spirit, the character, and the love of Christ coming out of us toward them.

We have made so many mistakes with our children (even carrying the "grace card"). But grace allows us to approach them openly and admit: "I was wrong. Will you forgive me?" That has spoken volumes to our children over the years. Recently Scott told us one of his most vivid memories.

> I was eight years old when I played on a basketball team at the YMCA. My dad was the coach. I was the leading scorer, so when I fouled out of a close game early in the fourth quarter, Dad was furious at the call and lost his cool, smashing his clipboard into several pieces. I was embarrassed along with the rest of the family. BUT after the game Dad found the referee and asked his forgiveness for his response. That made a big impression on me.

That's everyday parenting grace!

Build the Relationship
Without a strong relationship we will never impact our children positively.

The Apostle Paul wrote to Timothy: "The things *you* have heard *me* say" (2 Tim. 2:2, italics added). Obviously a strong relationship existed between Paul, the older, and Timothy, the younger. In fact, Paul viewed Timothy as his own son.

We can create *environment* and *example* in our homes when we have close personal relationships with our children. Love and communication in a discipling context offers the best mix for building a successful relationship with our children. Discipleship means investing in close personal relationships with our children and their friends. Friends are critical to the formula because they play such a significant role in creating the right environment for our children. Moreover, we have the opportunity to impact their friends' lives by bringing them into the environment of our homes. For example, when our children become teenagers, suddenly it's as if their parents contracted a disease. But we can befriend their friends, who'll think we are "cool." That's a huge factor in keeping open the relationship with our own children during their teen years.

[Only a healthy relationship will provide the opportunity to influence our children's lives positively.]

During their growing-up years, we worked with our children informally to help them grow in Christ. But in high school we had a discipleship group for them and their friends.

I met with Jonathan and his friends every Tuesday, 6:45 A.M. at Chick-fil-A on Lawrenceville Highway. We had basketball players and soccer players; some grew up in church and others did not. Some lived with two parents; some had parents who were divorced. One was brilliant, another had a learning disability. One friend, Tim, we had known since first grade. On his first visit to our house he had blown out the pilot light on our furnace (it was winter) and took our kids down the laundry shoot–all within thirty minutes after he arrived! All of them acted "squirrelly" and often forgot their books. "Where is your book?" I asked. "In my truck," one replied. "Would you get it?" I asked. "I looked, but I can't find it," he said. These interactions took place often. After we got a chicken biscuit, I began by saying, "Gentlemen, we're here to become men of God. Let's get started." Slowly they grew. Now they are in college. One spent a year as a missionary in Africa teaching English. Two served as youth interns at a church this summer. Each one wants his life to make a difference for Jesus Christ.

To make discipleship work, what *relationship building tools* do we need to create a superglue bond between our children and their friends and us?

Accept them where they are. Instead of trying to get kids to our level, get down to their level. That's as simple as bending down to talk to a smaller child at eye level. Or it's as complex as getting involved with a teenager on drugs and sticking with him until he is on solid ground.

Love them no matter what. Kids do things that irritate us to the point of mental meltdown. Teenagers particularly can get under our skin. Most adults have very little patience with kids. But that's what it takes. Ask God for the grace to love your children and others.

Don't give up on them. Sometimes I wonder: "Am I wasting my time?" It's easy to feel that when other kids, but yours in particular, aren't paying attention, don't seem to get it, and leave you feeling as if they would rather be someplace else. Yet I found that perseverance to continue the relationship, whether or not my children and their friends respond, is one key factor in success. It says, "No matter what you do, I'll never, ever give up on you."

Hang out with them. Go to their games. Get a milkshake. Shoot baskets or kick balls in the yard. Take in a movie. The list of fun, creative ways to spend time with kids is endless.

One word of caution, particularly to dads: Hanging out means getting in on their agenda, not getting them on ours. At the same time we can design events so that we hang out with a purpose. Carol and I have gone so far as to set up trips to national youth conferences and design trips to Eastern Europe for our children and their friends.

Only a healthy relationship will provide the opportunity to influence our children's lives positively.

Focus on Character

An environment of grace and a positive relationship allow us to enter into our children's lives. Once in, we can focus on character. Without grace and a relationship with us, our children will never learn character from us. But when those two elements exist, then developing our children's character becomes our primary focus.

> [What our children learn through difficulties does more to conform them to the image of Christ than anything else.]

People talk about character in many contexts today. So we need to define what we mean. From a biblical perspective we have character when we reflect the attitudes and actions of Jesus Christ. The Apostle Paul summarized it in 2 Timothy 2:2, using three phrases that speak about our character.

Faithful. We want our children to be "faithful." For years we have defined that using this **FAT** acrostic:

Faith-filled–trusting every situation in our lives to God
Available–flexible to be directed by God
Teachable–humbly eager to learn from God

Our immediate response: "I don't have any kids like that!" True! That's the challenge. Discipling our children means peeling back the layers of their lives and delving into their hearts, and then starting right where they are.

As a child, I had so much energy that I was bouncing off the walls. In sixth grade I received a paddling from Ms. "Duck" Neal *every day*. I still have scars in my arm and bottom from pencil fights I had in our youth group. A deacon in our church once told my dad, "Your son is either going to be a prisoner or a preacher. The verdict is still out on which one!" "Incorrigible" came much closer to describing me than "faithful." Nevertheless, my parents met me where I was with patience, love, and discipline. So wherever your children are, start there and trust God to change them and make them "faithful."

Entrust. God "entrusts" the faithful to communicate His character to others (2 Tim. 2:2). "Entrust" refers to a sacred trust. A safety deposit box illustrates it well. At the bank, if we want to get out our valuables, we bring our key and the banker brings his key. One key will not open it. It takes both keys. In discipling our children to passionately pursue Jesus, it takes the "key" of your life and the "key" of your child's life to open the riches that are in Christ. We enter this partnership in the Spirit to discover the character of Christ with our children.

Many witnesses. This phrase means that in front of many people and in many circumstances we have the opportunity to grow in Christlike character. Christ's character develops in our children only in the give and take of everyday, real-life situations.

As unpleasant as this is, our children often learn more about the Lord from the way we handle difficult circumstances than from "nice little Bible lessons" with pious, but untested, applications. In the last year Carol has been through colon cancer surgery and a skin and muscle disease, which have left her totally dependent. What a crucible for character building! As we left the hospital the other night, Ginny, our eleven-year-old, started to cry. I knew it was one of those precious moments. I rubbed her leg as I drove. We talked tenderly and prayed for her mom. We asked the Lord to help us keep our eyes on Him, not on the circumstances. She is learning to give her most precious relationship to the Lord. Nobody likes this suffering, but the Lord has drawn us closer to Him and one another. It's a part of God's goal to mold us to become like the Ultimate Pacesetter:

> I want to know Christ and the power of his resurrection and the fellowship of sharing in his sufferings, *becoming like him* in his death. (Phil. 3:10, italics added)

What our children learn through difficulties does more to conform them to the image of Christ than anything else (Rom. 8:29). The way we interpret difficult circumstances for our children will either turn them away from God or point them to Him.

How do we enter into a partnership with the Spirit using the circumstances of everyday life to help our children become faithful in expressing Christlike character?

• We *teach* our children through *instruction.* That happens in many ways, both structured and unstructured. We recommend teaching informally and in small doses. When children are younger, focus on breakfast devotions and bedtime prayers. Our goal is for our children to thoroughly understand the Bible, but more, to honor and love God's Word.

• We *train* our children through *skills.* As our children grow up, we can help them develop spiritual disciplines like Bible study, prayer, giving, witnessing, worship, fasting, and others. Don't count on them being particularly consistent with these disciplines. But at some point of maturity they will begin to own these.

• We *build* our children through *character development.* As we use every opportunity to apply God's Word to what they learn through teachable moments in real-life situations, character develops. We ask the Holy Spirit to create the kind of environment and example that encourages them to burn these applications deep within their hearts. As they do, they learn how to "trust in the Lord with all [their] heart and lean not on [their] own understanding; in all [their] ways acknowledge him, and he will make [their] paths straight" (Prov. 3:5-6). The goal is not to develop the character of their own natural personality, but rather to encourage the Holy Spirit to be so strong in them that they reflect the character of Jesus. No parenting course in the world can teach this. Only the Holy Spirit can build this kind of character in our children.

• We *send* our children out on *mission.* The character they develop needs to find expression. That can be anything from teaching a three-year-old brother to express love to his two-year-old sister, to sending a teenager to the other side of the world to share Christ with refugees. Being "on mission" deepens our children's convictions, creates a desire for more of Christ in their lives, and motivates them to express Him to others.

The test for Jonathan came his senior year in high school. During his junior year he had played soccer for his school. Surrounded by a good supporting cast, he had scored twenty-six goals, more than double the previous school record. He felt very good about himself. He expected his senior year to exceed his previous success. It didn't happen. Loss of players, the team's lack of motivation, and coaching changes all contributed to an unpleasant situation. Frustration mounted. Some teammates yelled at him, refused to pass the ball to him, and talked negatively to the coach about him. During one game his teammates and the coach were shouting at him, and then the coach took Jonathan out. That was it. Jonathan had had it. He walked off the field past the team up a hill, where he stayed. He didn't return. He didn't play the rest of the game. After the game we had a long, intense talk. He felt extremely hurt over the way he had been treated, but he realized that he had responded incorrectly. The next day he stood before his coach and the entire team to ask forgiveness. He played 100 percent for the rest of the season, making the best out of a difficult situation.

In a partnership with the Spirit and through a real-life situation, Jonathan's character grew, helping him become a more faithful young man.

This discipling process goes far beyond what most other parents or churches envision as part of their parenting responsibilities. Yet from God's perspective it is standard operating procedure. If we train our children in this way, then when they are old, they will not depart from it (Prov. 22:6).

Expect Multiplied Impact
Not only will your children not depart from the faith, but God will multiply their impact in the lives of others as well. Notice how that happens through Paul's pacesetting discipleship in 2 Timothy 2:2. "Paul…Timothy…reliable men…others also" shows the progression of influence that results from investing in people's lives. That same progression will take place in your family when you set the pace through discipling your children.

That has been God's grand design all along. It's hard for us to see the design as we go through the daily grind of dealing with our children. Carpools, soccer practices, paying bills, keeping up the house, and a myriad of other responsibilities can blur our focus. That's why we need to clarify God's ultimate goal for our children:

> Therefore go and make disciples of all nations,
> baptizing them in the name of the Father and
> of the Son and of the Holy Spirit, and teaching

them to obey everything I have commanded
you. And surely I am with you always, to the
very end of the age. (Matt. 28:19-20)

The mandate of the first disciples is still the mandate for
our children and for us. The tools given the first disciples
belong to our children and to us as well.

Power. Jesus told His disciples: "I have been given
complete authority in heaven and on earth." That authority
is like a police officer with a badge. If I go out to direct traffic, drivers will run over me. But when a police officer with
a uniform and badge directs traffic, everyone obeys. This
officer has the authority of the city, state, and nation behind
him or her. Jesus has "all authority" from His Father. He gives
that authority to us when we wear the badge of the Holy
Spirit. Our children have that spiritual authority.

Plan. The Great Commission hinges on Jesus' phrase:
"make disciples." Jesus put the emphasis on making disciples
because He knew that people in general, and our children in
particular, experience life change and become life-changers
through discipling. In addition, He knew that discipleship by
multiplication is the fastest way to change the world.
  If we *add* 1 + 1 = 2, then 2 + 2 = 4, then 4 + 4 = 8, and
8 + 8 = 16, and 16 + 16 = 32, we get the results of addition.
But if we take 1 + 1 = 2, and then *multiply* 2 x 2 = 4, then
4 x 4 = 16, then 16 x 16 = 1,056, and then 1,056 x 1,056 =
1,112,136, we get the results of multiplication. Discipling
multiplies. We want to give our children the vision that by
discipling one person per year, then in thirty-two years all six
billion people of the world's population potentially can be
reached.

Promise. The thought of mobilizing our children to take
the message of Jesus around the world is both scary and excit-

ing. Either way Jesus said, "I am with you always, to the very end of the age." Through discipling, the presence of God will enable our children to invest their lives in the extraordinary privilege of taking the Gospel around the world.

The week after Christmas I spoke to thousands of students in several cities. At my last stop I gave the final message at Reach Out's Christmas Challenge conference. By this time I had spoken so much that I was on automatic pilot. Punch my button and I popped up. At the end of the message hundreds of students responded. I looked at the scene in front of me: students in tears with their heads bowed, desiring to make a difference. I spotted my son, Jonathan, standing. Tears welled up in me, and I began to sob. It took some time for me to get my emotions under control. When I did, I spontaneously said to them, "I want to ask your forgiveness on behalf of my generation for leaving you the lousiest legacy in American history." (They did.) Then I told them, "I believe God is raising up you and your generation as the ones to finish the task of taking the message of Jesus around the world!" They began to clap and kept on clapping.

[God has called us to equip and then release our children for the incredible task of fulfilling the Great Commission.]

God has called us to equip our children for the incredible task of fulfilling the Great Commission. When we set the pace, they will respond, letting God use them for His Kingdom purposes. At least that's what we have experienced in our family.

Scott went to Duke University. He joined a fraternity with the express purpose of sharing the Gospel with his fraternity brothers. For four years he did that faithfully.

Several frat brothers came to Christ through Bible studies he led for them. His last semester his fraternity had a "Say So"–a meeting to say whatever they wanted to one another. Scott took advantage of this last opportunity to speak to his friends. Through tears he told them he wanted to leave them with his life philosophy: (1) to love the Lord with all of his heart, and (2) to love others. He told them how badly he wanted that for each of them. Kevin, his roommate, stood up afterward and said, "One thing I have known about Scott is that he loved me. He is the only person I know who has stood for his religious convictions and has not compromised." Scott and his wife, Cameron, are making plans to practice medicine in a foreign country to do their part to fulfill the Great Commission.

Katie attended Furman University. Her first year, a discipleship ministry began there. An older girl discipled her. During her sophomore and junior years, she lived on a freshman hall so she could share her faith with her girls and lead the interested ones in discipleship. Now the girls that she led lead their own discipleship groups. Katie married Bart Garrett, and together they want to plant a church where no one has ever planted one before as their part in fulfilling the Great Commission.

Jonathan joined a fraternity at Furman University for the express purpose of letting the light of Jesus shine. In the summer he worked at a discipleship and evangelism project learning more about his faith and communicating it to others. This summer he is taking a ministry team to Eastern Europe to equip and evangelize students. He wants to use his communication skills to fulfill his role in fulfilling the Great Commission.

Ginny, now twelve, still hangs out with Dad and is learning to love Jesus more every day.

When we set the pace, God will see that, in due time, our children will follow.

Taking Action

Using what you have learned in this chapter, set up your plan for discipling your children, including place, time, materials, and activities.

Penetrating Questions

1. Is Jesus Christ in your black box?

2. How would you describe the environment in your home?
3. How would you evaluate the example you have set for your children?

4. What are your major parenting weaknesses through which God wants to demonstrate His power?

5. On a scale of 1 to 10, how would you evaluate your relationship with your children?

6. What area would you pinpoint in which each of your children needs to develop character?

7. Will you make the investment to set the pace by discipling your children?

Fresh Ideas

• Describe in five phrases the positive and negative environment and example you have created in raising your children. On your knees, ask God to change any negatives into positives that will honor Him.

• Decide on one situation in which you need to use the "grace card."

• Design three inexpensive activities that will strengthen your relationship with your child.

• Create a plan for using mealtimes and bedtimes to communicate Christ to your children. Take their biggest need and pray for a specific answer. Memorize a Bible verse and then discuss what it means.

• Develop a structured discipleship time for your children and their friends using the discipleship resources described in the "Further Reading" section.

• Start praying daily for the multiplied impact of your discipling efforts. Begin now to ask God to use your children to help fulfill the Great Commission.

Further Reading

Henrichsen, Walter. *Disciples Are Made–Not Born*. Colorado Springs: Chariot Victor Publishing, 1974.

St. Clair, Barry. *Life Happens: Get Ready* and *Life Happens: Help Your Teenager Get Ready* will help in discipling older high school students. Nashville: Broadman & Holman, 1997.

St. Clair, Barry. The "Moving Toward Maturity" series, which includes *Following Jesus*, *Spending Time Alone with God*, *Making Jesus Lord*, *Giving Away Your Faith*, and *Influencing Your World*. These five, step-by-step discipleship books will provide you with everything you need to disciple fifth-grade through high school students. The *Moving Toward Maturity Leaders Guide* will tell you everything you need to do for success. Available through Reach Out Youth Solutions.

Sanders, J. Oswald. *Spiritual Leadership*. Chicago: Moody Press, 1967.

Break Through the Barriers

How do we work through our pain in order to avoid inflicting that pain on our children?

SUNDAY NIGHT I READ TO MY SIX YEAR OLD, Ginny, before praying and tucking her in. The phone rang. Our fourteen-year-old son, Jonathan, called from the car phone. He talked while his sister drove them home from a church in downtown Atlanta. At one point in the conversation I heard sounds like %^&%$#@##$$. At first it sounded like static on the line. Then I realized that it was glass and metal crunching. "Dad, we're in a wreck. We're in a wreck," Jonathan yelled. "Don't hang up," I yelled back. "Dad we've been hit. Katie is bleeding. She's cut." I could hear Katie, our seventeen-year-old, screaming. "Jonathan, get out of the car.

Can you get Katie out of the car?" "Glass is everywhere. Sparks are flying, and the car is rolled over on its top. I don't know if I can get us out or not!" "Jonathan, you have got to get out now!" After struggling, he pulled them both out. With fear running through my veins, I yelled, "I'm calling 911. Don't leave until I get there!"

With that I made the call and sprinted to the car. The normally twenty-minute trip took me eight minutes. When I turned the corner onto the street where the wreck occurred, lights were flashing all over the block. The emergency vehicles threw off enough light to make it look like daytime. Ambulances, fire trucks, and police cars covered the area. I sprinted to the scene. The first thing to catch my eye was our 1984 Sunbird turned upside down in a smashed heap–totaled. "Where are my kids?" ran through my mind. Then I spotted Jonathan wandering around in a daze. As I hugged him, I spotted a blood-soaked green sweater on the sidewalk to my left. I didn't have to guess whose blood that was. "Where's Katie?" "In the ambulance."

Again I sprinted, this time to the ambulance. Police and rescue workers crowded around the rear door. I pushed my way through, crawling on my hands and knees to my daughter. Blood covered her head and body. When we saw each other, both of us began to cry.

In the same way that Jonathan and Katie experienced that trauma physically, the younger generation has gone through severe pain and trauma emotionally, psychologically, and spiritually. The reason: the impact of the pain most of us have had to endure because of our parents. How far back does that pain go? All the way back to beginning of civilization. God spoke clearly to Moses when He gave the Ten Commandments:

> The Lord, the Lord, the compassionate and gracious God, slow to anger, abounding in love and faithfulness, maintaining love to thousands, and forgiving wickedness, rebel-

lion and sin. Yet he does not leave the guilty unpunished; he punishes the children and their children for the sin of the fathers to the third and fourth generation. (Ex. 34:6-7)

As parents, we can hurt our children. And our parents have inflicted pain on us. And their parents have wounded them. Clearly children pay for their parents' sins. If that pain is not addressed and dealt with properly, then it carries on from generation to generation. It becomes a major barrier in our ability to ignite the flame of passion for God in our children when we have not dealt with our own pain. That pain blocks the flow of God's love from us to our children.

How do we break through those barriers of pain?

Parent-Inflicted Pain

The wounds that parents inflict come in all shapes and sizes. Some hurts are so traumatic that they seem incomprehensible. They can kill a child's spirit. Others hurt deeply, but their wounds are not mortal. Still other wounds prick from the sparring of daily family relationships.

Violent wounds. After counseling with a very fragile looking fourteen-year-old girl, I received this note from her:

> I really want Jesus Christ in my heart. But there is one thing that really hurts me a lot. My grandpa molested me. He's been doing this for two years. My parents found out, but they don't believe me. But I told my parents: "Why should I lie?" I told my mom: "You just have to face it, because it is true." I stay up all night crying because this gives me great pain.

Only Jesus can bring healing to her. And only by confronting the reality of this issue can she get past the pain and not have a warped view of who Jesus really is.

Deep hurts. I liked Randy (not his real name). He was the first boy who ever took my daughter out. Those boys: You either like 'em or hate 'em! I liked Randy. He was sharp, friendly, and had a great sense of humor. Through the first couple of years of high school, he was in a discipleship group that I led for some high school guys. Then he discovered some things about his past that sent him into a tailspin. He began to dress weirdly, act strangely, and isolate himself from his friends. These signs reflected outwardly the deep wound he had experienced inside. He discovered that his father had left his mom when she was pregnant with him, saying he didn't want the responsibility of a child. The pain of that rejection created in him an overwhelming sense of grief that continued years later.

Randy knows where to find the answer. Like the Prodigal Son, he needs to return to the loving arms of his Heavenly Father. But without having had an earthly father to love him that is pretty difficult.

The devastating impact of these kinds of wounds is impossible to measure. But clearly they create the kinds of barriers that cause people never to reach their full potential, that create dysfunctional families, and that close off people from the intimacy of a relationship with their loving, healing Father.

All of those things were true of Richard. I met him first when he came to our church. He made an appointment with me to tell me that he was dying of AIDS. When I probed a little, he told me his story: Growing up, he was the All-American kid—athletic, popular, and an Eagle Scout. Then one weekend his older brother invited him to Atlanta. His brother had planned a wild weekend. Before it was over, his brother's friend had raped him. It devastated him. All he knew to do was to tell his parents, but they were extremely angry with *him*. A few days later he asked his father for the keys to the car. His dad tossed the keys to him and said, "Going out with some of your homo friends again?" It hurt him so much that he started a downward spiral of rebellion that in his words "left nothing undone. I did every perverted thing known to man." In the process he got AIDS. A few months later he died. The main reason: pain inflicted by his parents.

No Pain, No Gain
No matter how great a family we come from or how wonderful our parents are, we are going to get wounded in our family relationships somewhere along the way. In a very real sense all of us have wounds from our family.

What happened the night of the wreck as I cried over my Katie created an environment for our family to learn some precious and valuable lessons. Even though Katie was covered with blood, her condition was not serious. She had stitches in her head and hand and missed several days of school due to soreness. But the "minimum damage" done did not lessen the impact of the event or the significant lessons learned through this experience. I hope what we learned from the physical trauma will touch your life in the emotional and spiritual arena. Let's see how we can turn our pain into gain.

Call on the Wounded Healer
When I got to Katie in the ambulance, she was clutching her Bible in one hand. She grabbed my hand with her other hand. Through tears she told me, "Dad, I knew you were coming. While I've been lying here, I kept repeating over and over: 'Fear not, for the Lord your God will deliver you.'" Right there I thanked the Lord that He had delivered her and that He would continue to do so.

Looking at your life, where do you hurt? Behind the smile, where are the tears?

[Jesus is the only one who can deliver us *through* our hurts and tears.]

Jesus is the only one who can deliver us *through* our hurts and tears. He can do that because He is the Wounded Healer. Whatever pain has been inflicted on us in life, Jesus has been there and experienced it ahead of us. When we read Isaiah 53:2-5, we become aware of how true that is.

> He grew up before him like a tender shoot, and like a root out of dry ground. He had no beauty or majesty to attract us to him, nothing in his appearance that we should desire him. He was despised and rejected by men, a man of sorrows, and familiar with suffering. Like one from whom men hide their faces he was despised, and we esteemed him not. Surely he took up our infirmities and carried our sorrows, yet we considered him stricken by God, smitten by him, and afflicted. But he was pierced for our transgressions, he was crushed for our iniquities; the punishment that brought us peace was upon him, and *by his wounds we are healed.* (italics added)

- For those who feel ugly–He had no beauty.
- For those who have been rejected–He was despised and rejected by men.
- For those who have experienced deep pain–He was a man of sorrows and acquainted with suffering.
- For those who blame God for what has happened–He was considered stricken by God, smitten by Him, and afflicted.
- For those who have been beaten and abused–He was pierced for something He did not do.
- For those who have lost a child or other loved one–He was crushed by death.

Through the experience of the cross, Jesus went through every physical and emotional pain. He was scourged, which meant that Roman soldiers beat Him thirty-nine times with a whip entwined with sharp objects. He was spit on. They put a robe on Him and let the blood coagulate so that the robe stuck to His body. Then they ripped it off. They placed a crown on His head made of one-inch thorns, pressed it into His skull, and He bled profusely. The soldiers made Him carry His own cross. Then they nailed His wrists and feet with long spikes to the cross. Once nailed to the cross, the soldiers lifted the cross into its socket, which ripped His flesh. The pain was intolerable. Cicero called crucifixion "the most cruel and horrible torture." What scholars have declared the most horrible death ever invented by man, Jesus experienced to the fullest extent.

Many in Jesus' day were crucified. But Jesus went one step beyond the physical pain of crucifixion. On the cross He cried out with anguish beyond human comprehension, "My God, my God, why have you forsaken me?" For the first time since the beginning of eternity, Jesus was separated from His Father. At that moment His Father sent Him to hell–outside of the presence of His Father. Breaking this eternal bond of fellowship between the Father and the Son was the worst of all pains.

In the midst of our hurts and the need to be healed of them, what does Jesus' pain mean to us as parents? It means that He identifies with our pain. Wherever we have been, Jesus has already been there and beyond. Whatever our parents, spouse, or children have done to us, Jesus empathizes with us.

But going beyond that, He went through that pain so that He could heal our hurts. The Apostle Peter said it best:

> He himself bore our sins in his body on the tree, so that we might die to sins and live for righteousness; by his wounds you have been healed. (1 Peter 2:24)

To begin the healing process, Jesus wants us to admit our sinfulness, turn to Him, and let Him take away our sins. He wants to establish a relationship with us that will open the way for Him to bring healing into our lives and into our families. Then He wants to become the "balm of Gilead" to us. The Heavenly Father sheds tears for us and says,

> Since my people are crushed, I am crushed; I mourn, and horror grips me. Is there no balm in Gilead? Is there no physician there? Why then is there no healing for the wound of my people? (Jer. 8:21-22)

The Father sent Jesus to be that "balm of Gilead," who will deal with our pain.

We like the way Neil Anderson expresses it:

> Refuse to believe that you are just the product of your past experiences. As a Christian, you are primarily the product of the work of Christ on the cross. You are literally a new creature in Christ. Old things, including the traumas of your past, are passed away. The old you is gone; the new you is here. [Neil T. Anderson, *Victory over the Darkness*, Regal Books, 1990, p. 199.]

Start right here. Decide now that, whatever it takes, you will let Jesus come into those painful places in your life. Diagnose your situation and bring His healing touch. It is possible that your decision will break the cycle of generations of sin, broken relationships, and wrong behavior. That same decision creates the wonderful possibility that from this point on, your children and their children can live powerful, healthy, potential-filled lives. You can be the key that opens the lock to the Door, releasing all the wonderful things God has in store for you and your family.

Value Precious Relationships

Until the accident Katie and Jonathan picked on each other unmercifully. Only three years apart in age, they "duked it out" all the time. But this accident changed that. We did not discover until later that night–about 2 A.M. after spending several hours in the ER–that our son, Jonathan, was the hero. Not only did he have courage in the crisis to get himself and his sister out of a potentially explosive car, but also he took care of his sister afterward. Her blood-soaked sweater that I saw lying on the ground got that way because Jonathan had used it as a pillow to cradle Katie's head as he held her in his arms until the ambulance arrived.

> The people who hurt us the most are people to whom we are supposed to be closest.

Since that night their relationship has changed. They rarely fight. Instead, they have a deep love and respect for each other that wasn't there before. Jonathan even made the decision to go to the same college as Katie. Part of that decision had to do with wanting to be close to her. The accident showed them how much they value each other. They learned that their relationship is precious.

And so are ours! I have noticed that the people who hurt us the most are the people to whom we are supposed to be closest. Think about the hurts in your life. They did not come from the President of the United States not passing a bill that was important to you. You aren't angry because the voters didn't pass a school bond. You may be frustrated about those kinds of things, but your hurt and pain has come from family and friends. One of them did something (or several things) that has put a barrier between you.

I have one sister. Her name is Cathey. When I was sixteen and she was thirteen, I was working on a science project on our outdoor patio one afternoon. I asked her to get me a glass of water. Like a good little sister she did. When she brought it, I told her to hold it. "I'm almost through. Hang on." She wanted to put the glass down, and I wanted her to hold it. After a long while she became angry and poured the water all over my project. I slapped her across the face. She ran into the house, and I ran after her. I wanted to hit her again. Both of us were very angry.

It seemed from that point on, nothing I did for her turned out right. If I bought her something, it was the wrong size. If I tried to get her a date, the guy was a creep. Later she was going through some personal struggles, and in talking to our mom about it, she told her that I had been a crummy big brother. When my mom told me about that, it broke my heart. I didn't know what to do, but I realized that I had to do something. I went to my sister's place, and we sat on the couch to talk. "Cathey, I have been a crummy big brother to you," I told her. I listed eight or ten examples. Then I asked, "Will you forgive me?" She sat there poker-faced for what seemed like an eternity. Then big tears welled up in her eyes. We slid across the couch to each other. When we hugged, the barriers between us finally came down. She said, "I forgive you."

Interestingly, within six weeks of that time, I was able to help point her in a direction that got her headed toward solving her situation. Often I have thought, "What if...what if I had said, 'She's just my little sister.' Or what if I had said, 'It's not that big a deal.'" It could have radically altered my sister's life (and mine) in a negative direction. More importantly, because both of us dealt with the pain, we were able to re-establish the closeness we had before.

How do we keep from erecting barriers that separate us from each other? Our family adopted these words from the Apostle Peter when our kids were in high school. We memorized them and talked about them in numerous "sticky" family situations. This is how God wants us to value our precious relationships:

Finally, all of you, live in harmony with one another; be sympathetic, love as brothers, be compassionate and humble. Do not repay evil with evil or insult with insult, but with blessing, because to this you were called so that you may inherit a blessing. (1 Peter 3:8-9)

Count 'em. In these verses there are at least five actions we can take to increase the value of precious relationships:

- Be sympathetic.
- Love as brothers (and sisters).
- Be compassionate.
- Be humble.
- Do not repay evil actions and insults.

We found that putting them into practice daily minimized the hurt and maximized the health of our relationships with one another.

Pray Hard for One Another

Earlier on the evening of Katie and Jonathan's accident, Carol and I had gone to a fellowship meeting with some couples in our church. Our kids had gone downtown with their friends to a church service. After a meal and conversation, we divided the men and the women. Each group went into a separate room to pray. In the men's group we prayed for our children. Normally the men's group is a rather quiet bunch, praying silently. We prayed for each of our children. Then we began to pray for God's protection over them. With more and more intensity and volume we prayed for the Lord to watch over them. We prayed for them by name. Then I did for our children what Moses told the Children of Israel to do. I prayed the blood of the Lamb over the doorposts of their cars. We were into it. It was not a dull prayer meeting!

Not an hour later I was on the phone with my kids when

the wreck occurred. Later I found out from the police officer that if the Lincoln Continental had hit on Katie's side six inches closer to the door instead of the *doorpost* of the car, she would have been killed!

God was protecting our kids that night—no doubt about it! And God wants to protect each of our families, too. He has given us many promises about His desire to do that. One we like very much is:

> The Lord watches over you–
>> the Lord is your shade at your right hand;
>> the sun will not harm you by day,
>> nor the moon by night.

> The Lord will keep you from all harm–
>> he will watch over your life;
>> the Lord will watch over your coming and going
>> both now and forevermore.
> (Ps. 121:5-8)

Not only does He want to protect our families physically, but emotionally, relationally, and spiritually as well. Satan is out to destroy our families. Watching him try to poke holes in our family, I have noticed that he does it where we are the weakest. Often that is in our relationships. He likes to drive a wedge between us with hurt feelings, not getting what we want, being treated insensitively, or rubbing another person the wrong way. As parents, our job is to pull out any wedge that exists within the family. This must be dealt with on a spiritual level. The Apostle John, the writer of Revelation, put it this way:

> For the accuser of our brothers,
> who accuses them before our God day and night,
> has been hurled down.
> They overcame him

by the blood of the Lamb
and by the word of their testimony;
they did not love their lives so much
as to shrink from death. (Rev. 12:10b-11)

Begin to pray now for your family, that Satan will be overcome. You don't want him to have the slightest foothold in your family. Pray that the blood of Jesus will heal and protect your family. He will overcome any damage Satan has caused in creating wounds and hurts in your family. He will do that through your prayers!

Pray that the blood of Jesus will heal and protect your family.

Offer Forgiveness Freely

One of the struggles I had the night of the wreck, especially when I did not know how badly my children were hurt, was my anger toward the driver of the Lincoln. I had never met him, but I did not like him! I had to deal with forgiving him for what he did to my kids.

Forgiveness is extremely hard to do. Only followers of Christ can find it in themselves to do it. No question—God wants us to forgive those who have hurt us. Jesus made that exceedingly clear:

For if you forgive men when they sin against you, your heavenly Father will also forgive you. But if you do not forgive men their sins, your Father will not forgive your sins. (Matt. 6:14-15)

When we choose to forgive, it does not mean that we choose to let the other person run over us. It *does* mean that we are choosing to let God, the just Judge, work it out His

[**No question—**

God wants us

to forgive

those who

have hurt us.]

way (Rom. 12:19). We offer forgiveness. God brings justice.

We may say, "That person hurt me so badly that I can't forgive him." But if we don't forgive, then the pain we feel will not only continue, it will get worse. Forgiveness is the only way to let go of the past and stop the pain.

So how do we forgive?
1. Decide now to be honest. God wants to bring these things into the light so they can be dealt with.
2. Write the names of the people who have hurt you.
3. Beside their names, write down what they did to cause you pain. Be specific.
4. Write how you feel about these people and the hurt they have caused you. Don't bury your feelings. The only way to forgive from your heart is to know what is in it.
5. Bring all you have written to the cross. Jesus took on the sins of the world—that includes yours and the sins of the people who have offended you. The cross is the place of true forgiveness.
6. Decide to forgive. You probably don't feel like making this decision, but this is not about feelings, but obedience. Since God tells you to do it, He will give you the power to choose to do it.
7. Pray this prayer: "Lord Jesus, I choose to forgive (name) for (the offenses). I forgive him or her just as You forgave me. In Jesus' name, Amen."
8. Destroy your list. You are now spiritually free. In time your emotions will catch up.
9. Don't expect change in the other person.
10. Try to understand the person you have forgiven by praying for him or her according to Matthew 5:44.

11. Accept your part of the blame for the offenses you suffered. If that caused pain for someone else, go to that person and ask forgiveness. Say this: "I was wrong. (List the ways.) Will you forgive me?"
12. Thank God for what you have learned. Write those lessons down. [Adapted from Neil Anderson, *Victory over the Darkness*, pp. 203-5.]

If we follow this process, we can experience healing from the hurt, get on with our lives, and not create relational and emotional gaps in our lives that will keep us from loving our children and being the kind of parent we need to be.

Both my wife and I come from healthy families. But because of wounds experienced outside of our families, we have needed God's healing power to make us whole. As a result we have prayed for those with hidden, hurtful memories to find healing. One person we have prayed for is Sally. She came from a home with an alcoholic mother. Her father left the family in her junior high years. The sense of embarrassment over her mother's drinking and the loss of her dad created deep wounds. One afternoon she opened up to us about her family. She had never told anyone before. That began the healing process that continued over time. As a result of her healing, her brother came to Christ. Together they began to pray for her mother. She accepted Christ and never touched alcohol again. Sally forgave her dad, too, and went to him to reconcile the relationship.

As wonderful as this was, Sally recognized that she still has leftover anger from living in such a dysfunctional home. Often she directed that anger toward her children. In a time of intense prayer, the "balm of Gilead" soothed her wounds, bathed her in love, and replaced anger with a deep sense of God's love and acceptance. Over time she has created totally new ways of relating to her children. She has entered into the process of turning woundedness into wholeness.

As we respond to God concerning the pain in our lives,

then in time we will be able to think about the people who wounded us without feeling hurt, anger, or resentment. Now we can parent our children as a *whole* person. That means we have a *whole* lot more to offer!

Taking Action
After answering the seven *Piercing Questions*, take the steps of obedience needed to give and receive forgiveness.

Piercing Questions
Think about one of these questions each day for the next week.
1. What is the one major hurt your parents have inflicted on you?
2. Why do you think Jesus can be the Wounded Healer to you? (Review Isa. 53:1-6.)
3. What does your family do that lowers the value of relationships and keeps your relationships from being precious to each other?
4. How do you need to pray for your family?
5. Who do you need to forgive in your family?
6. Are you willing to forgive that person?
7. Will you walk through the steps of obedience necessary for you to experience forgiveness?

Fresh Ideas
Use any of these ideas to help you move from woundedness to wholeness.
• Identify any sin that has dominated your extended family. Trace it through your family tree as far back as you can.
• Write your name on one side of a sheet of paper and Jesus' name on the other side. Make a list of all the wounds you have experienced and then directly across the page write how Jesus experienced that same hurt.
• Draw across on a sheet of paper. Bring all of your wounds

to the cross by writing down the names and offenses of people who have hurt you. After you forgive them, burn the paper.

• Record, in writing, your decision to let Jesus be the Wounded Healer to you.

• Write 1 Peter 3:7-8 on a poster for your family. Ask them to tell you how you can value ("honor") your relationships more. Ask them what they are willing to do, not what they want others to do.

• Place a sheet in your Bible or notebook that has the names of each family member on it and the issues you are praying about for each one. Divide the sheet in half so you can keep prayers on one side and answers on the other.

• Write the names of any people you need to go to and ask forgiveness (Matt. 5:23-24). Write down what you will say to them. Go!

Further Reading

Anderson, Neil. *Victory over the Darkness*. Ventura, Calif.: Regal, 1990.

Mayhall, Carole. *Words That Hurt, Words That Heal*. Colorado Springs: NavPress, 1993.

Nouwen, Henri. *The Wounded Healer*. Austin, Texas: Image Books, 1979.

Seamands, David. *Healing for Damaged Emotions*. Colorado Springs: Chariot Victor Publishing, 1981.

Tap Into the Right Resources

How can we rely on God's supernatural ability to raise our children?

RUNNING VERY LATE FOR THE PLANE, Bill and I made a mad dash down the long escalator at the Atlanta airport. We ran for the train that would take us to the plane. If we didn't catch that train, we had no chance of catching the plane. As we ran toward it, the train door began to close. I was ahead of Bill, so I lunged for it. The door closed on me. "No problem," I thought. Surely it would work like an elevator door and pop open. NNNNNNOOOOO! Wrong answer.

Half of my body was wedged inside the train, and half of it hung on the outside. The inside half consisted of one arm–with a briefcase, one leg, and my head. The outside half included my other arm–holding a suitcase, and my other leg extended in the air. The train door had creased my body and was beginning to cause me pain.

Then the nasal, robotic R2D2 voice intoned over the loudspeaker: "The door will not close. The door will not close. Someone is caught in the door. The train cannot leave while someone is in the door." I wanted to yell, "That's me, stupid. I'm the one. You caught me. Way to go. Now get me out of this jam!"

In desperation I looked for some help in this train full of people. Each one stared at me, eyes communicating: "You idiot! You look stupid in that door." No one took a step to help me. Clearly I was stuck, and if the train took off, I would be dead. Bill stepped in and saved me. He pried the door open, and both of us hopped onto the train.

That comedic picture of me in that door is the picture of most parents trying to raise their children. One side of us tries to raise our children using limited parenting skills, saying to ourselves, "I should be able to handle this." However, after our son has hit his little sister for the tenth time in the last hour, another side of us realizes that we need help beyond ourselves—the help of God's resources. Rely on my skills or trust God's supernatural abilities? It's not a hard call, but it's still easy to get caught in the door.

If this issue didn't impact our children so powerfully, then we could move on to "more parenting nuts and bolts." But it makes a huge difference. Even with superior parenting skills we cannot:

- open a child's heart to receive Christ
- change a pouting, whining, screaming child into one at peace
- root rebellion out of a teenager's heart
- create a sense of purpose in life
- cause our children to live for Christ

Only God can do those things.

Certainly it makes sense to apply the wisdom and insight we have learned through experience, but our Heavenly Father's desire is for us to submit our parenting abilities to Him and let Him take control of parenting our children.

What difference does that make? On the one hand, a direct correlation exists between relying on *our own abilities* and our children living their lives by *extrinsic motivation*. On the other hand, a direct correlation exists between relying on *God and His resources* to raise our children to live by *intrinsic motivation.*

RELYING ON MY PARENTING ABILITY ⟶ EXTRINSIC MOTIVATION

RELYING ON GOD'S RESOURCES ⟶ INTRINSIC MOTIVATION

Outside the Door–Relying on Our Own Resources

Naturally we get hung up on how we want our children to turn out. We have this picture in our minds of what they will do, how they will act, and who they will turn out to be. We take this approach, often unknowingly, instead of seeking to understand what God's picture is for their lives.

Where did our picture come from?

From our parents. Often the only picture we have for raising our children is the one our parents have given us. Because all of us have imperfect parents, that has both positive and negative points.

From our insecurities. Because we don't want our children to embarrass us, we enforce rules on them that ensure that their behavior conforms to the standard behavior of other children. This can seem to work well when our children are younger, but when they become teenagers, it gets really messy.

From our false view of success. Because we want our children to turn out "right," we have all sorts of ways to modify their behavior–from rules to shaming, from a rewards system to bribing. We believe this will shape and mold their lives. And it does—only negatively instead of positively.

The world outside our homes gives our children plenty of "ammo" for wrong things to do. If we are protective parents, as we should be, we want to shield them from those wrong influences. However, some parents make a grave error in not protecting their children from the "right" things too–grades, position on the team, friends, social status, and material things. We think that for our kids to be "successful," they have to "do well" and "have" certain things. Doing the "right things" can be as destructive as the "wrong things." Both approaches place us outside the door–relying on our own parenting skills and producing in our children extrinsic motivation.

Note: Some parents are permissive either by design or neglect. The laissez-faire approach to parenting is simply irresponsible. We are continually amazed at the parents who take this approach, providing no guidelines and little significant input into their children's lives. Taking this parenting stance is definitely "outside" the door of God's resources. We will address this issue in Action #6 on setting limits. Since you have taken the initiative to read this book, in all likelihood you are not a "hands-off" parent.

Prisoners in Our Own Homes

Why do we get stuck "outside the door," trying to motivate our children externally?

The Apostle Paul addressed that issue in his letter to the Galatians. Paul spoke to the extrinsic motivation issue raised by a group of people called Judaizers. They believed the rules of the Old Testament were binding on the New Testament church. Their complaint was that Paul had removed from the Gospel certain legal requirements in order to make the message more appealing to the Gentiles. They insisted that Gentile converts had to abide by the Old Testament rules.

This was extrinsic motivation at its highest level.

The Apostle Paul emphatically responded by telling these extrinsic motivation gurus that they were deserting God by insisting such a thing:

> I am astonished that you are so quickly deserting the one who called you by the grace of Christ and are turning to a different gospel–which is really no gospel at all. Evidently some people are throwing you into confusion and are trying to pervert the gospel of Christ. (Gal. 1:6-7)

At the heart of Paul's argument is extrinsic motivation–achieving by our own efforts. That has no connection whatsoever to the Gospel of Jesus. In fact, it is the world system coated with religion. Most commonly it is known as legalism. Bottom line: It is man trying to please God through human effort. From the first century on, extrinsic motivation in the form of legalism has run through the church like a stinking sewer. And it still flows through the church today. We need to understand it as parents and get as far away from it as we can.

The implications of this can have an extremely negative effect on the family. It makes us prisoners in our own homes. When we try to raise our families through human effort, we experience three devastating effects:

1. No one is acceptable to God because we can never reach His standard.

2. Therefore, we are never acceptable to one another either, because we can never possibly measure up to one another's standards.

3. Carried out in practical living, over time, we make

ourselves and our children people-pleasers instead of
God-pleasers.

Those effects make us "prisoners...locked up" said the
Apostle Paul (Gal. 3:23). When we parent our children with
this philosophy, our families are trapped!

Three Parent Traps
When we get trapped like this, most of the time without even
knowing it, it shows in three very real ways.

Guilt. If we hear ourselves often saying, "You ought
to...you should...you could," then we know that we are
inducing guilt. It's the kind of guilt that causes us to feel as if
we will never quite do it right.

Take Allen, for instance. He grew up as a "military brat."
He had used drugs in high school, but then Jesus turned his
life around. Since then, he has completed college, is married,
has three beautiful children, and is a successful school
teacher and youth leader. But he has always struggled with
never feeling as if he was good enough. When he discovered
that these feelings came from his father, he tried to talk to his
dad about it. His father's response: "When I was thirty-nine,
I was successfully starting my second career. You are thirty-
nine and haven't even started your first." That hurts! The
years of "oughta...shoulda...coulda" guilt his dad put on
him coupled with this final devastating blow caused him to
write his dad off.

Nothing positive came from that! Imagine how that
impacted his relationship with his children.

Fear. We instill fear in our children resulting from our
own fear. When fear drives us, then our method is rules.
When children break the rules, we punish them. (Notice we
did not say discipline. See Action Point #6.) Fear reasons this
way: "If we don't have strict rules, then our kids will get into
sex, drugs, and alcohol." Fear results in overreaction. Then
our kids react to our overreaction. In this cycle not enough

restrictions exist in the world to keep a kid from rebelling.

A couple talked to me about their teenage daughter. The way they described their situation with their daughter, I thought they had a little hellion on their hands. When they brought her to talk to me, I met this sweet, nice young lady. Something wasn't adding up here. I asked the dad what the problem was. He replied, "She plays this loud music." I asked him what they had done about it. He said, "Well, because she won't do what we asked, I grounded her for three years." My reaction: "Three what!" For a teenager three days is a life sentence. Three years is eternity.

When the crime does not fit the punishment, we know we have served up a fearful overreaction.

Performance. How easy it is to fall into the performance trap. It communicates: "You are not measuring up to my standards."

All five blue uniforms were huddled in a bunch around the basketball. Wherever it went, all five of these little girls in the blue uniforms followed it. One of the girls in a blue uniform was our ten-year-old Katie. She had decided to try basketball for the first time. This was the first game. We watched in agony. I (Barry) had played basketball in college. So after the game, I told her that we were going to learn some things to help her. Later, on the court, I instructed her: "Katie, get the ball and drive to the basket." Every day we worked on getting the ball and driving to the basket.

The next Saturday the same girls in the blue uniforms hovered around the ball, and my Katie was right in the middle of them. I told Carol, "She is not getting the ball and driving to the basket." Then I said to Katie, "Get the ball and drive to the basket." That fell on deaf ears. So I yelled to her, "Katie, get the ball and drive to the basket." It still did not happen. So I stood up and yelled louder, "Katie, get the ball and drive to the basket." She stopped in the middle of the floor, put her hands on her hips, and yelled back, "Dad, I'm trying to get the ball and drive to the basket." The gym fell dead silent. Everyone stared at me. Total embarrassment engulfed me.

Old Dad had taken his years of basketball know-how and tried to impose it on his sweet and unsuspecting little gal. She had no clue. The possibility of her measuring up to my standard was totally zero.

I did that so naturally. And that is the point. We naturally gravitate toward performance, guilt, and punishment in the way we handle our kids. What God wants is for us to move toward the supernatural. Then we can function in a new dimension of parenting.

> We naturally gravitate toward performance, guilt, and punishment in the way we handle our kids.

Emotionally and spiritually extrinsic motivation (based on guilt, fear, and performance) leaves our children and us feeling empty. It creates negative responses from everyone. And in the long run it creates the opposite effect from what parents desire.

Have you ever wondered why so many teenagers pack their bags to go to college or get a job, and when they walk out, they leave the "religion" bag behind? Why do so many of them who grew up in church go absolutely berserk when they get away from home–drinking, using drugs, and having sex? Of course, there could be many reasons why they rebel, not the least of which is that they are going their own way because of their own choices. However, many come through what we call "the tube" of religion at home and at church. They see the extrinsic motivation–guilt, fear, and performance–all in the name of religion. They want nothing to do with it. They have gotten sick and tired of boring, empty, meaningless exercises that produce no significant life-change. In most cases this response is the very opposite of what we had hoped. But most of our kids want to throw open the door and experience life on a fresh, new level. We can open the door for them. How do we do it?

Inside the Door–Relying on God's Resources

How much richer and deeper our parenting experience will be if we raise our children by tapping into the supernatural power of God. By doing this we move away from surface Christianity into a real relationship with Christ and with one another. It's our only viable alternative.

No one has expressed more clearly how we can live by God's resources than the Apostle Paul:

> I have been crucified with Christ and I no longer live, but Christ lives in me. The life I live in the body, I live by faith in the Son of God, who loved me and gave himself for me. I do not set aside the grace of God, for if righteousness could be gained through the law, Christ died for nothing! (Gal. 2:20-21)

To sort that out in simple terms:

- Jesus died and was raised up from the grave.
- When I receive Him, I die to my selfish desires, and the resurrected life of Jesus is infused into me.
- Now Christ lives in me to strengthen, empower, and enable me to live the way He desires.
- If I could have done this for myself, then Jesus' death was needless. He died for nothing!

[**Grace: God's supernatural ability working in me through the cross and the resurrection.**]

All four of these statements are contained in the meaning of the word "grace." Let us offer a concise definition of grace: God's supernatural ability working in me through the cross and the resurrection.

Grace is like bookends in all of Paul's letters. He begins each one talking about grace and ends each one the same way—except for Romans; and that *entire* book is about grace. Take the above definition and use it anywhere you see the word "grace" in the New Testament, and you'll find that it fits perfectly.

In his argument against the Judaizers in Galatians, Paul unlocked the prison door with the "grace" key. Grace unlocks the prison door, which frees us from raising our children with fear, guilt, and performance. Grace leads us into the sunshine of *intrinsic motivation*. As we apply it to our family, we can see that it creates at least three extremely positive effects on us and on our children.

1. We are acceptable and pleasing to God simply because we have the Spirit of Christ living in us (Gal. 2:20).
2. We can rely on the Spirit of Christ and all of His resources rather than on our own abilities (Gal. 5:16-18, 22-23).
3. Carried out into practical living, God builds into our children and us a desire to be God-pleasers rather than people-pleasers (Gal. 1:10).

The result: We are free, and our children are free (Gal. 5:13). Isn't that what our goal is? We want to move them from dependence to independence. Freedom is what they want more than anything else. Amazingly they already have it. Our parental job is to teach them how to use it by tapping into God's resources.

Working that out practically with our kids is tricky at best. Consider this very personal illustration.

Scott, our oldest son, had his learner's permit. He played

on a basketball team that practiced across the city. Three afternoons a week I sat on the passenger's side as he drove back and forth in the Atlanta traffic to practice. One principle of driving that he had not yet conquered was the proper use of the brakes. When the brake lights lit up on the car in front, instead of applying his brakes, he would accelerate. We had spoken of this several times. I would explain, "Scott, one day you will not stop in time, and you will hit a car."

One afternoon after practice we were cruising along. Suddenly the brake lights of several cars came on, but this time they stopped more quickly. Scott slammed on the brakes–hard. Tires squealed. The smell of burning rubber filled the air. I grabbed the dash and prayed out loud, "O Lord, help us." God answered that prayer. We missed the car in front of us by half an inch or less.

I looked over at Scott. His hands were shaking, and his face was white as a sheet. He mumbled with a trembling voice, "Dad, I think you'd better drive." We switched places. On the way home we stopped to get a burger and gather our wits. We talked it over. As we walked out of the restaurant, I headed toward the driver's side of the car. Then I stopped dead in my tracks. "Scott," I said, "here, you drive." I tossed him the keys.

That, ladies and gentlemen, was the grace of God in action! My natural response was "Choke the boy!" Furthermore, I would never have thought of tossing those keys on my own. It spoke volumes about how I had grown in this area, because grace is rarely ever my first response. I could have easily defaulted to extrinsic motivation by applying fear, guilt, and performance to this situation. "Scott, you could have killed us, and if you had, it would have been your fault. You are a terrible driver. If you don't improve, I won't ever be able to let you drive again." Instead, I was intrinsically motivated–I was led by the Spirit to toss him those keys. My response was the difference between a negative and positive learning experience. And we gained the added benefit of becoming closer as father and son.

The contrast between extrinsic motivation resulting from fear, guilt, and performance and intrinsic motivation resulting from God's grace becomes huge when we begin to apply it to raising our kids. For example, in Ephesians 2:8-10, the Apostle Paul created a beautiful picture of what grace does in the lives of our kids:

> For it is by grace you have been saved, through faith—and this not from yourselves, it is the gift of God—not by works, so that no one can boast. For we are God's workmanship, created in Christ Jesus to do good works, which God prepared in advance for us to do.

What does God do when He applies grace to our families?

He saves us. He saves our children. He draws them out of sin and death and into a personal relationship with Jesus that gives them life. We have parents ask us all the time, "Is it too late for my family? My kids are so messed up. We have made so many mistakes." That is the wonderful thing about grace. It is never too late. And the problems are never too big. God's supernatural ability through the cross and resurrection can save the day and redeem the situation. That gives all of us imperfect parents, who have raised imperfect kids, hope!

He designs our children to be the "unique work of art" they were destined to be. That is the literal translation of Paul's phrase in Ephesians 2:10. "God's workmanship" means "His unique work of art." In a world where kids tend to become culture-clones, where they all look weirdly alike, God's grace causes them to discover their total and absolute uniqueness from every other human who has ever lived. And then His grace shows them their unique destiny that only they can fulfill. (See Action #7 for an in-depth discussion.)

We have the opportunity to make the paradigm shift away from relying on our abilities and begin to tap into the resources of God's grace. What a difference that makes!

Windows to Look Through

You may say, "I don't know whether our family has opened the door and jumped into God's grace or not." Let's peer into four windows to see whether or not grace is operating in your family.

Window #1–Gratitude

When we operate on performance, then no one ever measures up to the standard. Therefore, not only do we gripe and complain, but also we create an environment that encourages our children to gripe and complain. We expect others to meet our needs. When they don't, we let them know it. Often "the greater the affluence, the less the gratitude." Many kids with more don't appreciate what they have. But when grace operates in a family, no matter what their economic status, then deep appreciation prevails. That gratitude is based on what Jesus did for us on the cross. By His *mercy* we don't get what we do deserve. By His *grace* we do get what we don't deserve. Therefore, we can have a thankful attitude for every circumstance in our lives. Grace creates "an attitude of gratitude" in our homes.

Window #2–Transparency

Fear, guilt, and performance from extrinsic motivation drive us to hide from our real selves. People don't feel free to tell the truth. At home we tiptoe around issues, knowing that no one wants to deal with them honestly. Yet when grace kicks in, we take off our masks. Like the Apostle Paul, all of us have a "thorn in the flesh." We can try to hide it, or we can be honest about it. Paul's openness brought this response from God: "My grace is sufficient for you, for my power is made perfect in weakness." Paul, continuing the theme of transparency, responded to God, "Therefore I will boast all the more gladly about my weaknesses, so that Christ's power may rest on me" (2 Cor. 12:9). Grace allows us to expose our weaknesses. When we take the lead in doing that, our kids will be transparent too.

Window #3–Conviction

Extrinsic motivation forces our convictions on our kids. When they reject those convictions, we get upset–like the dad who called me one night. His anger made the phone rattle.

"John came home wearing an earring today," he said, seething.

"Is that a problem?" I asked.

"It's the worst thing he could have done, and I am kicking him out of the house," he replied in a loud voice.

"What's wrong with it?" I continued, knowing full well that it went against every fiber in his body. "Is it immoral, unethical, or illegal?" I asked.

"No, but it's not right!" His anger was still rising.

We talked through the issue. I tried to help him see that the earring was not the real issue, but *why* John wanted to wear it. He had a reason for it, and John's dad needed to discover it. I knew enough about the situation to understand that this dad had forced his views on his three boys for years in very demanding and unloving ways. It was the epitome of extrinsic motivation.

I explained to him, "God's grace is so much better. John needs to develop his own convictions through God's Word and the Holy Spirit, rather than your jamming them down his throat. This approach will motivate your son internally, causing him to want what God wants, and therefore what you want." This dad never got it, and he and his son are still estranged.

It doesn't have to be that way. Through God's grace we can help our kids develop their own convictions. How do we do that?

Window #4–Trust
What if, like John and his father, parents and children choose different convictions? Extrinsic motivation doesn't allow for that. It's "my way or the highway." "Either adhere to my rules and hold my values, or you're out of here!" The reason for fear, guilt, and performance is that parents don't trust their children with God or God with their children, particularly in their teen years. Without trust, the only option is to establish a rule for every situation. How many rules will we need? We don't have enough paper to write them all down.

Yet through grace, we trust God with our children and our children with God. For example, let's say you believe in Christ, as does your eighth-grade son. In that case…

- Does the Holy Spirit live in you? (Yes.)
- Does the Holy Spirit live in your eighth-grader? (We could debate if eighth-graders have souls! Just kidding. Yes.)
- Then why do you play the role of Holy Spirit and tell your eighth-grader everything to do? What to wear? Who to have as friends? What to believe?

Before you think we've gotten weird, stick with us. If the Holy Spirit lives in you…and in your child, can't the same Holy Spirit speak to both of you? "He's not mature enough to hear," you protest. Tell that to Joseph, Samuel, David, and other young men in the Old Testament. Because "God is no respecter of persons," why can't you trust God to work in your child's life, as you expect Him to work in yours?

Catch this point because it is the heart of intrinsic motivation. From early on you want your children to respond to God. How can they do that if you always tell them what to do? Can we relate to our children in a way that helps them discover for themselves what God wants them to do? This doesn't mean we don't discipline our children. (See Action #6.) But it does mean that the focus of our discipline, rules, conversation, and all other ways we relate to our children is teaching them how to hear the voice of God, rather than just following our directives. If we trust the Holy Spirit who lives in their embryonic human spirit and appeal to Him, then over time and experience God will make them "strong in spirit" like John the Baptist–the person Jesus described as the greatest human who ever lived (Luke 7:28).

Our goal, therefore, is intrinsic motivation that causes our children to become "strong in spirit." Then they will possess the inner convictions to make Spirit-led decisions in any moral, social, and spiritual climate.

Buttons to Push

What practical steps can we take to bring the grace of God into the daily reality of our families' lives and cause our children to grow up with the intrinsic motivation of the Holy Spirit? Pushing these buttons will open the door to God's grace and keep it open.

Button #1: Decide now to open the "grace door."
We need to decide about the grace issue. All other parenting issues will flow from this one. This decision will determine how we operate as a family. Once we admit our inability to raise our children on our own and make our desire to raise them by God's grace, then we have chosen God's path. That decision will open many other doors for our families. The psalmist spoke of the value of that decision:

> You have made known to me the path of life;
> you will fill me with joy in your presence,
> with eternal pleasures at your right hand.
> (Ps. 16:11)

If this is a fork in the road for you, make this significant decision now.

Button #2: Pray the "grace prayer" daily.
We pray this simple "grace prayer" daily for our children. It reminds us of whose ability we rely on.

> Lord, I can't. You never said I could.
> But you can. You always said you would.

Write that prayer on a card. Place it in your wallet, on your dinner table, and on your refrigerator door. Pray it out loud. Utter it under your breath. Pray it when things are going well. Use it to plead with God when things are falling apart. Make it your "parenting prayer."

Button #3: Share the Gospel with each of your children.
We have had the privilege of leading three of our children to Christ. That is the starting place for applying God's grace to them. Don't worry about your ability or experience in doing this. He will convict them "in regard to sin and righteousness and judgment" (John 16:8). His job is to draw them to Himself. Our job is to explain the message. We used a booklet that we read to them. (See "Further Reading" at the end of this chapter.) Then we asked them if they wanted to pray a prayer to accept Jesus. A few days later we had our children write their testimony. These were some of our greatest privileges and most thrilling moments.

Jonathan used the same booklet we used with him to talk to his youngest sister Ginny. She wrote this testimony:

> "Lord, I can't. You never said I could. But you can. You always said you would."

> In the winnter when i was six my brother Jay read "The Facts of Life" to me. That night while Jay was babysitting me, I invited Jesus into my heart. Now I know Jesus and I want to love and follow Him the rest of my life.

If your children are not open to accepting Jesus now, keep praying for them, loving them, and sharing with them. In time, they will want to know Him because of your example.

Once our children have begun a relationship with Christ, they will be able to respond to God's grace because God's Holy Spirit's living in them will enable them to do so. That makes your job much easier!

Button #4: Appeal to the Holy Spirit in your children.
We try to catch ourselves when fear, guilt, or performance becomes our mode of operation. When we say, "You ought to...you should," we stop ourselves and then turn that statement into a question: "What do you think God is saying to you about that?" When one of the kids hits another one, naturally we want to say, "You ought not hit your sister!" But turning that into a question, we ask, "What do you think God wants you to do about hitting your sister?" That question takes the issue from extrinsic motivation–parents' values externally dropped on this child–to intrinsic motivation–this child has to decide internally what God wants him or her to do in this situation.

We try to use each opportunity as a teachable moment. We talk about what God says and what His response would be. If they don't know what they are doing is wrong or what God says, then we take time to help them discover one or both and respond correctly.

[**Ask the question: "What do you think God is saying to you about that?"**]

Using the question, we appeal to the Holy Spirit in our children. Repeated over and over during their childhood, our children will develop their own convictions given by the Holy Spirit and based on God's Word.

If we appeal to the Holy Spirit in our children on the smaller issues when they are young, then they will learn to respond to the Holy Spirit on the larger issues when they get older. Over time they will become "strong in spirit" because they will develop their own intrinsic motivation based on the Holy Spirit living in them.

When we push these buttons daily, we tap into God's resources. Our experience has shown us that when parents do that, they will see three significant results in their children as they grow:

1. Strong self-image.
2. Sexual purity.
3. Setting limits through proper discipline.

We will discuss these issues later in this book. In fact, from here on each chapter will help you throw the grace door open wider and wider.

As we close the door of fear, guilt, and performance and open the door of God's grace, our children's lives will change dramatically. In years to come, we will know that our parenting ability did not cause the change. Rather, we will say, "God's grace changed my children." Both you and your children will know that the fire of passion in them for Him came from His grace.

Taking Action

Open the door to God's grace by pushing the four buttons discussed in the chapter:
1. Decide to open the grace door.
2. Pray the grace prayer daily.
3. Share the Gospel with each of your children.
4. Appeal to the Holy Spirit in your children.

Piercing Questions

1. In your own experience what one example illustrates how you have relied on your own parenting skills?
2. What examples come to mind that show how you relied on God's grace with your children?
3. What is your picture of each of your children? How does that differ from God's picture?
4. In your view how has guilt, fear, or performance negatively affected your children?
5. On a scale of 1 (low) to 10 (high), how would you evaluate these "grace windows" in your family?

Gratitude   1 2 3 4 5 6 7 8 9 10

Transparency 1 2 3 4 5 6 7 8 9 10

Conviction   1 2 3 4 5 6 7 8 9 10

Trust   1 2 3 4 5 6 7 8 9 10

6. Will you throw open the grace door for you and your family?
7. Will you pray the grace prayer daily?
8. Will you share (or have you shared) the Gospel with each of your children?
9. In what situation can you use the question "What do you think God is saying to you about that?" with your children?

Fresh Ideas

• Determine the trigger point when guilt, fear, or performance traps you personally. Ask the Lord to heal that weakness by His grace.

• Evaluate the trigger point when guilt, fear, and performance trap your children.

• Do a Bible study on grace. Look up all the verses in a concordance. Read one at each evening meal.

• Prepare a Gratitude Box. At the evening meal, ask each person to write one blessing your family has but doesn't deserve. Put it in the box until it is full.

• Use The Ungame questions to promote transparency.

• Give the grace prayer to your family. Decide how you want to do it–frame it, laminate it, or put it on a magnet.

Further Reading

The Good News Glove (for leading your child to Christ). Orlando, Fla.: Campus Crusade for Christ, 1971.

Lucado, **Max**. *In the Grip of Grace*. Dallas: Word, 1996.

McGee, Robert. *The Search for Significance* (book and workbook). Houston: Rapha, 1985.

Piper, John. *Future Grace*. Sisters, Ore.: Multnomah Books, 1995.

St. Clair, Barry. *The Facts of Life*. Atlanta: Reach Out, 1986, 1999.

Swindoll, Charles. *The Grace Awakening*. Dallas: Word, 1990.

Yancey, Philip. *What's So Amazing about Grace?* Grand Rapids, Mich.: Zondervan, 1997.

Build an Intimate Home

**How can we build an environment
of unconditional love in our homes?**

DURING THOSE CRAZY DAYS when nothing seemed to go right (which can be every day after children arrive), we would hide out in our room and design our dream house. Carol would pick up the *Southern Living* house plans at the grocery counter, and later we would daydream about a larger kitchen, an efficient laundry room, and a bathroom with "his and her" sinks.

We never moved, but we remodeled twice. After the first bout with chaos, dust, and dirt, we were hesitant to create more confusion. But as we looked at the living conditions, we knew it was time. Katie and Jonathan shared what we called "the red, white, and blue" room. As they grew older, it grew fuller. They decided it was time to take the bunk beds apart and at least have separate space, which they did. However, that did not settle the growing tension about which part of the room belonged to whom. One day it came to a boiling point. We heard the commotion and waited. Finally, Katie stomped into the kitchen–mad. She announced loudly, "I am now a teenager. I need my privacy. Since you won't do anything about it, I have. I divided the room with masking tape!" "So where is Jonathan?" we asked. "He can't get out of the room because the door is on my side," she explained.

The next day we placed the long-overdue call to the builder. The six-month mess started again in order to create the right physical structure for our family's living environment.

In the same way we had to build on to our house in order to create the right environment–parents need to build an environment of intimacy at home. That intimacy environment centers around our deep affection and God's unconditional love. If we miss that, then putting into practice all of the other chapters in the book cannot make up for it. However, once we build intimacy, then our children have to choose to receive it. We can never demand that they do.

A builder goes through four phases in building a house to produce a "turn-key" job. We must go through those same four phases in order to create an environment of intimacy in our homes.

What are the four phases that build an environment of intimacy?

The Foundation: Love in the Spirit

When we got married, we were madly in love. Soon after the honeymoon, however, the realities of life together took over. At that point, love became a choice, a commitment–not just a romantic feeling. How sad when married couples reach the conclusion: "We don't love each other any more." If you are

losing your grip on your love for each other, consider carefully a phrase we have prayed for each other for years:

…love in the Spirit. (Col. 1:8)

That phrase moves us beyond our meager capacity to
love and offers us the possibility of loving others with God's
love. How does it work? Both of us have
seen the flaws in each other. Because those
flaws can irritate and frustrate us to distrac-
tion, we decided that instead of focusing
on the flaws and trying to change each
other, we would ask the Lord to give us His
supernatural love to express to each other.

To "love in the Spirit" we need to be
"filled with the Spirit" (Eph. 5:18). Turning
away from our sinful attitudes and actions
toward each other and asking God to fill our
spirits with His Spirit has released His love to
flow freely through us. Loving in the Spirit
can overcome any problem in marriage.

[The greatest gift we can give our children is to love our spouse.]

Loving in the Spirit creates a desire to
meet the needs of the other person. The first
result of being filled with the Holy Spirit is
that we "submit to one another out of reverence for Christ"
(Eph. 5:21). That attitude continually connects us with each
other and recreates a unity between us. The result: We have
stayed madly in love with each other.

submitting to one another

The greatest gift we can give our children is to love our spouse. That love provides a powerful sense of security for our children. The husband/wife relationship hinges on love and respect:

> However, each one of you also must love his wife as he loves himself, and the wife must respect her husband. (Eph. 5:33)

Love and respect in a marriage creates an environment that makes it much easier for our children to "honor" and "obey" us and for us to bring them up "in the training and instruction of the Lord" (Eph. 6:4).

Our marriages need to model this kind of intimacy for our children. The way we model that for them will affect the way they relate to others, especially in dating and later in marriage. In our relationship we have discovered three cause-and-effect principles that lead us into deeper intimacy.

Love leads to physical affection. It does not work the other way around. Barry and I stood in the kitchen smooching. Twelve-year-old Jonathan walked in and exclaimed, "Gross me out!" As he walked out, he smiled. Our children will sense the love between us when we express physical affection. They learn how to express proper affection to others as they see us express it properly.

Forgiveness leads to conflict resolution. Suppose Barry walks in and sees that the house is a disaster. (With younger children this is a most likely scenario.) Instead of helping solve the problem, he blurts out, "Carol, the house is a wreck." (This has happened.) To say the least, that hurts my feelings. Tears flow. Tension fills the air. To resolve that conflict, he must ask forgiveness. That goes so much deeper than saying, "I'm sorry." It centers on having a humble and repentant attitude and saying, "I was wrong for not under-standing all you have been through today, for speaking out instead of helping out, and for not considering your feelings.

Will you forgive me?" When our children see submission in action and hear forgiveness being asked for and given, they will understand how to handle conflict themselves.

Lifetime commitment leads to security. A few years ago several couples we knew were getting divorced. We noticed Katie, then ten years old, was pensive and worried when we talked about those couples. She didn't want to talk about it. When we probed further, she burst into tears, crying, "I'm afraid you will get a divorce like those other people!" We sat down with all of our children, looked each one in the eyes, and said with confidence, "We love each other deeply. Because of the commitment we made to God and to each other, we promise you, we will never get a divorce." They gave a big sigh of relief and an even bigger hug. The subject never came up again.

Loving in the Spirit is a growth process. Through some very real tension and then honest conversation we have learned to ask ourselves these questions. They have helped us evaluate how we are doing in loving in the Spirit.

Do we **accept** *each other without reservations or expectations?* When we first married, Barry thought I should run as much as he did. At six miles a day, he had unrealistic expectations. I did not want to run at all. We had to learn to accept each other and lay aside our expectations.

Do we **adapt** *to each other's desires?* I like to arrive ten minutes early. Barry doesn't like to leave until it is time to arrive. Every outing we have to work hard on the EDT. Both of us have learned to give, change, and adapt.

Do we **admire** *each other openly?* For us, that means not taking each other for granted. Everyone likes positive accolades. We are no different. We have learned to hand out large doses of "You really handled that situation well," "I'm proud of what you did," or "You look really nice today." Sincere admiration positively encourages the other person.

Do we **appreciate** *each other by listening to each other?* One way to know we have stopped appreciating each other is when one of us says, "You're not listening!" That often comes from digging in our heels, saying, "I know I'm right." At other times we get so busy that we don't take time to talk and listen to each other. Both of us feel appreciated when we say to each other, "I want to know what you think and feel."

Do we **act kindly** *toward each other?* Nothing fans the flame of intimacy more than sacrifice. Driving carpool when the other's schedule is overloaded or flexing the eating schedule are but a couple of examples of the myriad ways we take action to help each other. Those not-so-random acts of kindness elicit great warmth from both of us toward each other.

Dealing with these questions not only helps us love each other practically but also models to our children how they can lovingly respond to us and their siblings.

You can be madly in love! All it takes is a few sparks prompted by the Spirit to get the fire going. When it is going in your marriage, it will spread to the rest of your family.

[**Build your marriage on Ephesians 5:18-33, and your marital woes will decrease significantly.**]

The Frame: A Healthy Marriage

The strength of the structure of our home has come through finding and then fulfilling our God-given roles in marriage. When we counsel couples in premarital counseling, the first assignment is always to study thoroughly Ephesians 5:18-33 and explain the roles of the husband and wife. If every couple built their marriage on these principles, marital woes would decrease significantly.

How does a husband stay in love with his wife? The daily grind and the frustration of unmet expectations cause wives to want to escape. James Dobson has identified eight avenues women can take to escape:

1. Detaching herself from her home and family with an outside job.

2. Expressing feminine anger at "male chauvinist pigs."
3. Remaining at home in quiet desperation and depression.
4. Entering an affair to meet her needs.
5. Turning to alcohol and/or drugs.
6. Trying to commit suicide.
7. Denouncing her responsibilities and walking out.
8. Seeking a divorce. [James Dobson, *Straight Talk to Men and Their Wives*, Word, 1981, pp. 99-100]

How can we build a healthy marriage so our wives won't be driven to these kinds of responses? The Apostle Paul tells us what to do in Ephesians 5:18-33.

• *Stay filled with the Holy Spirit (v. 18)*. As we learned earlier the Holy Spirit is the love solution in all relationships!

• *Submit to our wives (v. 21)*. All of my life I have heard it the other way. "I thought the wife was supposed to submit," we protest. So why do we submit? Because we follow Jesus and Jesus was a servant leader (Matt. 20:26-28). Submission isn't forced. It is initiated by the one who submits, not the one submitted to. God put us into the marriage to meet our wife's needs. If we can submit, we can serve. If we can serve, we can meet her needs. What kind of needs?
—Building self-esteem
—Relieving from the daily drudgery
—Providing adult companionship
—Giving romantic love
  Only serving by submitting can meet those needs!

• *Serve as her responsible protector (v. 23)*. The husband is "the head" of the wife. That does not mean that men are dictators, that women are inferior, that we make decisions with no discussion, or that we are always right. Rather, serving as "the head" means that we take responsibility for our wives rather than taking control of them. That responsibility means that we have an awareness, a sensitivity, and a burden for our wives. The word "head" actually means covering, like putting an umbrella over someone when it rains. God has given us the privilege of protecting them.

• *Sacrifice for her as Christ sacrificed his life for the church (vv. 25-27).* Someone has said to husbands, "Our home is not our castle; it's our Calvary." When we choose to sacrifice for our wives, we take the kind of action that brings out her full womanhood. Sacrifice brings fulfillment to our wives in three specific ways: Sacrifice *sanctifies* her, meaning literally "to put her to the proper use." Her proper use is to help her husband and in so doing bring beauty to his life. Nothing makes a woman happier than knowing that she has entered fully into her husband's life. Therefore, we need to open our hearts and lives to our wives. Sacrifice gives her *splendor*. Far beyond the way we would take care of an expensive sports car, we need to take care of our wives, because they have such value. One significant way to do that is always to honor her in front of others. Sacrifice removes her *scars*. Those scars come from worry, fear, anger, irritation, bitterness, jealousy, and stress. When we sacrifice for our wives, those scars disappear!

• *Specialize in tenderness (vv. 28-30).* Most men don't naturally love their wives tenderly. But it can happen supernaturally. God has given us the privilege to "nourish" them. To do that we must give positive attention to their relationship with God (spiritual), their feelings (emotional), what they are thinking (mental), and what they are doing (physical). That pretty much covers the waterfront. When we give that kind of focused attention, they will move from one stage of maturity to another in every area of their lives. Also we have the opportunity to "cherish" our wives. Cherish means "soft and tender like a mother bird over her young." Men tend to be harsh. As a result women tend to resist us spiritually and sexually. Women need tenderness. When we give it, they openly share every part of their lives with us. To "nourish" and "cherish" we need to have our wives in mind continually as we tenderly look out for their best interests.

Loving our wives like that will not only create a security in them, but it will also cause them to love us even more.

How does a wife respond to her husband?
With a husband like the one described above any woman will respond positively. What does her response need to be? The Apostle Paul in Ephesians 5:22-24 and 33 says wives are to "submit" and "respect." We have noticed that people have a knee-jerk reaction to both of those words when it comes to marriage.

- "I refuse to be a doormat."
- "That's not fair."
- "I've got rights."
- "I'm not going to wear a ball and chain."

Without trying to defend a position, we simply want to state what the Bible says and affirm that it has worked beautifully in our relationship. "Submitting to one another out of reverence for Christ" has been a linchpin that has held our marriage together.

Husbands and wives are equal but different. Both men and women were created "in the image of God" (Gen. 1:27). In Christ we are all equal (Gal. 3:25-28). However, it is easy to get equality mixed up with authority and roles. To have order in our homes we need an authority structure just as we have in business. The organization of our homes looks like an umbrella. God is the Ultimate Authority. Under His cover, therefore, the husband, the wife, and the children follow. To discover more about this you can study 1 Corinthians 11:3, Ephesians 5:18–6:4, Colossians 3:18-21, and 1 Peter 3:1-7.

Only submission and respect will cause your husband to reach his full potential. Wives have a profound influence on their husbands and children. When a wife does not submit and respect him, the result in the marriage and family is devastating. It creates:

- An attitude of resistance in the family
- An eroding of confidence in our husband's ability to make decisions
- A resentment concerning his past failures
- A bitter attitude about ways he has hurt us in the past
- An attitude of rebellion in the children
- A failure to build loyalty on the part of the children toward the family
- An inconsistency in the way the children are disciplined
- An inability to be involved in our husband's work
- A lack of enthusiastic sexual response
- An effort to control our husband's conscience, instead of letting the Holy Spirit do that

Only submission and respect will lead to oneness. A wife's total oneness with her husband comes as a result of submission and respect. Jesus was totally one with His Father (John 17:23). They had a *dynamic oneness.* The reason for that oneness was that Jesus always did what pleased His Father (John 8:29). He submitted to His Father's will (Matt. 26:39), and He respected His Father in a way that caused Him to do what His Father wanted Him to do (John 5:19). In the same way Jesus related to His Father, wives are to relate to their husbands.

I (Carol) am not by nature a rebellious person. My most rebellious moment growing up was when my daddy told me to change out of my cowgirl outfit, and I stomped and screamed. But when I married Barry, my rebellion came out. We moved to Squaw Valley, California, to start a church a week after we were married. I found myself not wanting to do any of the things he asked me to do. Through lots of tears the Lord showed me my rebellious self as well as the places where Barry was frustrating and irritating me. During that long, hot summer, I faced my rebellion and began to learn to submit to God by submitting to my husband. That turning point for me paralleled Barry seeing his selfishness and beginning to sacrifice to meet my needs.

We were in the middle of discovering these things when Barry got a call from a family we did not know who had just arrived by bus and found the name of our church in the phone book. They had come to beautiful Lake Tahoe because they knew that was where "Bonanza" was filmed! They had uprooted the family and brought their meager belongings with them on the bus. They called us expecting us to take care of them.

The newly married St. Clairs had quite a heated discussion about what to do. Finally, after tears, we decided I would fix dinner for them (submission), and Barry would make sure they did not invade our small honeymoon suite that already had two other guests Barry had invited to come and see us in California (sacrifice). I tried to cook venison that someone had given us. I had never cooked venison before, but I tried (submission). Barry ate it and said it was good (sacrifice). Later that night when we got those people on their way, we went to a little dessert place and talked through what had we had learned (love!).

Wives can do anything, go for any goal, accomplish any task, and hold any position as long as she is at one with her husband through submission and respect. It will take you toward your maximum potential. So go ahead and try it. It will drive your husband absolutely crazy–and he will love you for it. So will your kids!

The Furnishings: Cozy Togetherness

Not unlike your home, in the St. Clair household days extend into weeks when we zip here and there feeling overwhelmed by activities–work, church, ballgames, piano lessons, gymnastics, and on and on (it's tiring to even read the list). It's not hard for our homes to become places people pass through on their way to someplace else. We need to create a sense of cozy togetherness in our homes that allows us to step back from the fast-paced world. Often we ask ourselves how we can make our home a comfortable, peaceful place. The writer of Proverbs tells us:

> By wisdom a house is built,
> and through understanding it is established;
> through knowledge its rooms are filled with
> rare and beautiful treasures. (Prov. 24:3)

What special treasures need to furnish our homes so they become places of cozy togetherness?

Make Jesus Christ the centerpiece. Jesus is the one who brings security, significance, peace, joy, warmth, and love into our homes. Concentrate on putting Him at the center of your home so that everything else pales in comparison to His presence. Here are some ideas that have helped us do that.

• We place a Bible on our table, read it aloud, and talk about what we learn around our meals. It's not what we would call a devotional. It's just a conversation. A question like: "How about giving us a Bible verse and then telling us about it?" gets the conversation started. If nobody has anything to say, don't sweat it. Tell them one thing God has done in your life and move on.

• We take an issue that one of our children is dealing with, and we pray together about it. That may take thirty seconds or thirty minutes. The focus isn't how long it takes, rather how often we do it. We make a habit of praying with our children about all of their concerns, both big and small. We've found that we rarely run out of something to pray about.

• We pray with each of our children before they go to bed at night. We have found that to be a special time of closeness with each other.

• We have our own time alone with God. We try to do that early in the morning to establish our focus for the day. By placing Jesus first in our lives over the years, our children have caught the value of that. Now it's quite rewarding to walk in on our teenagers and see them kneeling by their beds with the Bible open in front of them.

• We have a brief time together to pray and read the Bible. Honestly, this has been one of the hardest areas to stick to consistently due to our often hectic schedules. But we have never given up.

• We take Communion together as a family. We learned this from the Prices, Carol's parents. They do that every day in their home. When they do, they pray for each of their children and grandchildren. What a heritage!

When Jesus is the centerpiece, then everything else will find its proper place in due time. Cozy togetherness begins right here.

Create family guidelines. Cozy togetherness will quickly vanish without "house rules" being established. Without rules, chaos reigns. People yell and scream at each other; sarcasm and criticism fill the air. Each person does his own thing, often to the detriment of the other family members. With each added family member, the confusion intensifies. Because of the distress caused by the lack of clear guidelines, family intimacy is threatened. However, when those guidelines become firmly established, the entire family can operate in harmony.

[
FAMILY

GUIDELINES:

respect,

honesty, and

obedience
]

In our home we have narrowed the guidelines down to three. Stated negatively they are *disrespect, dishonesty,* and *disobedience.* But let's state them positively, because that is the way we want to advertise them at home.

1. Respect. Any parent who leads at church must "see that his children obey him with proper respect" (1 Tim. 3:4). That respect originates with parents respecting each other and results in the children following suit. In speaking to teenagers, we give them practical ideas on how to show respect. These go both ways. Apply and teach these, and they will help build respect:

- Refuse to yell.
- Express appreciation—"Thanks for ..."
- Talk regularly.
- Seek their advice.
- Enter their world.
- Pray for them daily.
- Confess wrong attitudes regularly.
- Say "I love you" often.

2. Honesty. When family members speak "the truth in love" (Eph. 4:15), then honesty prevails. Kids want to be trusted. But when lying creeps in, then no one can be trusted. Nobody knows who or what to believe. Lying will quickly erode the entire family communication structure. That's why our family policy is: "No matter how bad it hurts, keep all the cards on the table." Honesty leads to honor. They are the same root word. If we want our children to honor us, then we must be honest with them.

3. Obedience. We teach teenagers to "obey your parents in the Lord, for this is right" (Eph. 6:1). We tell them that if Dad says, "Don't date for a year," then it is just like the Lord saying, "Don't date for a year." Obedience has four facets to it that make it complete:

- Do what you are told.
- Enjoy it.
- Figure out the positive reasons why you are doing it.
- Look for ways to do it better.

In our home anyone violating any of these three guidelines receives severe disciplinary action. Other negative behaviors that usually consist of innocent mistakes receive only kindly spoken verbal correction. When they follow these guidelines, then God promises "that it may go well with you and that you may enjoy long life on the earth" (Eph. 6:3).

Add a touch of hospitality. A home that exudes intimacy opens its doors to others. An open home that draws in a variety of people creates a center of fun and action. When our children become teenagers, they enjoy hanging around the house because that is where the action is. The sacrifice of giving up bedrooms, preparing meals, and cleaning up the messes is a small price to pay to have the reputation of being the place where the action is.

Take the visit from our cousin Price, for example. He lost his eye to an arrow as a child and had it replaced with an artificial one. Our children were drawn not only to his stories about his experiences with one eye but also to his fascinating collection of pocketknives. It seemed that for each knife he had a story about how the Lord had done something special in his life. We kept trying to scoot the children off to bed. Katie, eight at the time, kept slipping back into the living room. When we insisted that she go to bed, she responded, "But, Mommy, don't you know this is how little people learn?" Now married and in her own home, Katie is hooked on hospitality herself. One day her kids will enjoy the same kind of action-oriented home she had.

When school, peers, and cars begin to draw your children away, don't panic. After a while they will sense an even stronger drawing back to the place of love–back to home. And even better, when they begin to entertain thoughts of marriage, they will desire to find someone who can help them build a home like the one they came from.

The Finishing Touches: A Museum of Memories

An atmosphere of intimacy grows into a vast collection of treasured memories. In the future when your children reflect on their childhood, they will have certain memories. Over the years they will collect a whole museum of either positive or negative ones.

Edith Schaeffer described these memories in a classic book on home and family:

> Memory! What a gift of God. And what a tragedy at times. Memory can be of horrible things one wants to forget, coming at times like a nightmare trembling of horror, or memory can be of wonderful things one enjoys living and reliving. Memory can bring sudden understanding later in life. . . .
>
> What is a family meant to be? Among other things, I personally have always felt it

is meant to be a museum of memories—a collection of carefully preserved memories and a realization that day-by-day memories are being chosen for our museum…and that time can be made to have double value by recognizing that what is done today will be tomorrow's memory. [Edith Schaeffer, *What Is a Family?* Fleming H. Revell, 1975, pp. 189-91]

We build memories from day-to-day experiences. When we asked a class of parents what they remembered as special times with their own parents and family, it was often the simple, yet caring, expressions of everyday life:

- "My father helped me learn to ride my bike, running along beside me."
- "My dad sat in the stands for all of my ballgames."
- "Going to the library as a family and quietly reading after we had all found a book."
- "Getting a package of cheese crackers and a drink in the snack shop after a nervous visit to the doctor or dentist."
- "When I was sick, my mama would feel my head to see if I had a fever. I will never forget her hands."

Notice that the positive memories all centered on times when they felt physically close to their parents, when they felt special to them, or when they felt grateful for time spent.

How can we start now to build our own museum of memories from our daily experiences?

> We build memories every day.

- Recognize opportunities to say "I think you're special" with a small gift or note.

- Use the bedtime routine of bathing, snuggling, reading, singing, and praying.
- Turn a regular meal into a picnic surprise.
- Attend your children's practices and activities with a camera in hand.

As our children get older, we can add events that create memories.

- Use the bedtime routine for back rubs and relaxed talks.
- Leave love notes in lunch bags and backpacks.
- Take your kids and their friends or their dates to their favorite restaurant.
- Invite their friends to an after-the-ballgame pizza party at the house.
- Take a group of friends on a spring break or summer vacation trip.

We can go beyond the daily activities and plan for special memories. Shirley Dobson writes:

> The great value of traditions comes as they give a family a sense of identity, a belongingness. All of us desperately need to feel that we're a family that's conscious of its uniqueness, its personality, character and heritage, and that our special relationship of love and companionship make us a unity with identity and personality. [Shirley Dobson and Gloria Gaither, *Let's Make a Memory*, Word, 1983, p. 14]

Those special memories often come in the form of traditions. Some of those are quite natural like birthdays and holidays. The St. Clairs have quite a collection of memories built on birthdays:

- A superman party with eight boys dressed up in towel Superman capes, one Lois Lane (sister Katie), and a big "S" cake.
- A dress-up tea party complete with homemade chocolate eclairs. No boys allowed.
- A treasure hunt with clues all over the neighborhood leading to a treasure chest with surprises for everyone.
- A trip to Atlanta's finest restaurant for a dinner date with Dad on Katie's thirteenth birthday.
- An all-over-the-city extravaganza with guys and gals crammed into two vehicles for Katie's sixteenth birthday.
- A Hawaiian luau bash in September to celebrate Ginny's birthday in December because the hoopla of Christmas takes the luster off of her special day. Ginny planned this one herself—her eleventh.
- A "This Is Your Life" for Barry's fortieth.
- A surprise for Carol's fiftieth that was the party of all parties. This took several months of preparation with Carol's friends, who created committees for food, program, facilities, video, scrapbook, and so on. People came from all over the country to honor Carol. It was awesome!

Holidays open another avenue to create memories. For us, Christmas wouldn't be Christmas without the Christmas Eve candlelight dinner, the "Jesus' Birthday Cake" (an ice cream cake), and our special family program. "Christmas morning is a bonanza for everyone" Barry writes, "because Carol is the world's number-one Mrs. Claus. She goes all out to make it the best day of the year for our kids. Never have we come away without a special surprise from her creativity. Last year she had a special charcoal sketch drawn of our home, because it was our twenty-fifth anniversary of living there. Then she had a copy made and framed for each of the children so they could have it as a lifetime keepsake!"

Every holiday has its own special decorations, meals, and

plans. Thanksgiving brings out Grandma's dress-up pilgrims and our centerpiece of pumpkin gourds and fresh vegetables, football games, sleeping, and hanging out. Valentine's Day includes every meal in red with special Valentine decorations, including the scented tissue flowers. Easter celebrates Jesus' death and resurrection with hunting plastic eggs filled with a nail, a thorn, a cross, spices for Jesus' body, and a cotton ball for the Lamb of God. On Labor Day, our last big fling as a family before school starts, we used to participate in our annual neighborhood road race and then go out for a huge brunch with friends.

Family trips have produced some of our most pleasant memories. We can measure the impact of the trips by how many years the funny stories get told over and over again. For our vacation we have a place in Florida, where we go every year. Anytime the word "vacation" comes into anyone's mind, that is the place we think of. We enjoy it so much that when we are getting too stressed, we fantasize about it as our escape. What do we do? Nothing much! We sleep, swim, eat, sleep, work puzzles, play tennis, play games, sleep, ride bikes, talk a lot, and sleep. We want to go right now!

Individual trips taking only one of the children provide an incredible opportunity to give focused attention. For instance, last year I (Barry) spoke in California and arranged to take Ginny with me. We spent ten days together. Five of those were in my world and the other five in hers. Her five days we did the big things: Disneyland (a picture of Ginny, Pooh, and Dad sits in a prominent place in her room), Knott's Berry Farm, and Sea World. Yet some of our most memorable times were the unexpected experiences. Like the day we drove down to Balboa Island. A friend had gotten us a "nice" car. When we got it, however, it had no air conditioning, and he mentioned that the electric windows "might be having problems." They were. We tried to ditch that car and get a rental car, but my driver's license had expired five months earlier. I couldn't get a rental car, but we still had "the wreck." We drove it down to sophisticated Balboa Island. When we parked it, indeed, the windows did not work, nor did the doors open, except for one. To get out of the car Ginny had to climb out the window and unlock the hatch-back so I could get out. The first time it wasn't too bad, but by the end of the day we were ready to drive that car into the ocean! Ginny still remembers! That trip built a special bond between us that will last a lifetime. We have done that with each of our children. Taking trips has proven to be one of the most significant memory builders of all.

All of these memories have been thoroughly documented in picture albums and journals (more than twenty volumes at this time) so that our children have a museum of memo-ries now as they start their own families.

When you build on the solid foundation of love, frame your home with a healthy marriage, furnish it with cozy togetherness, and put on the finishing touch of wonderful memories, the plans for an intimate home inevitably will become a reality.

Taking Action
Ask your spouse which one of the four home-building phases you need the most work on, and then determine your two steps of action to work on it.

Penetrating Questions
1. How has your love grown or diminished toward your spouse over the last few years?

2. Are you filled with the Holy Spirit (Eph. 5:18)? If not, ask the Holy Spirit to fill you now.
3. What do you think that "loving in the Spirit" can do for your spouse and children that loving in your own strength can't do?
4. Since the greatest thing we can do for our children is to

love our spouse, what practical actions do you need to take to express more love to your spouse?

5. How would you rate your marriage in these areas? (1 is dead, 3 is alive, 5 is Olympic shape)

Affection	1	2	3	4	5
Attitudes of forgiveness	1	2	3	4	5
Assurances of security	1	2	3	4	5
Accepting	1	2	3	4	5
Adapting	1	2	3	4	5
Admiring	1	2	3	4	5
Appreciating	1	2	3	4	5
Acting kindly	1	2	3	4	5

What one action will you take to change your weakest area?

6. How do you view your role in your family? How does that differ from what the Bible teaches? What can you do to get your attitudes and actions in line with God's view?

7. Is Jesus Christ the centerpiece of your home? If so, how does that express itself? If not, what steps do you need to take to make Him the centerpiece?

8. What guidelines do you need to build harmony into your home? Which one will you implement with your family this week?

9. What is your happiest memory in your museum of memories? Tell your family about it before the day is over.

Fresh Ideas

- If you are struggling with loving someone in your family, write out a prayer you will pray for that person based on

Colossians 1:8.

- Talk to someone you know who radiates Christ. Ask that person to help you grow in your understanding of how you can love in the Spirit.

- Do a Bible study with your spouse on Ephesians 5:18–6:4. Use it as a platform for discussion on each one's roles and how you can carry out those roles more effectively. Listen to each other and don't try to defend your position when you talk.

- Set aside a two-hour time period to make practical decisions about how to make Jesus Christ the centerpiece your home, what guidelines you need, and how you will introduce those to your family in order to create more harmony.

- Plan one special experience this month that will build a memory in your family. Plan an experience *they* will enjoy.

- Attend a marriage retreat with your spouse.

- Set aside a weekend to trace your heritage. Find those in your family who have followed Christ over the generations. If you can find no one, then pray about how to start a Christian heritage beginning now.

- Put together an heirloom book of memories using journals and pictures.

- Read and discuss some of the books listed below with your spouse.

Further Reading
Dobson, Shirley, and Gloria Gaither. *Let's Make a Memory*. Waco, Tex.: Word, 1983.

Harley Jr., Willard F. *His Needs, Her Needs*. Old Tappan, N.J.: Fleming H. Revell, 1986.

Hybels, Bill and Lynn. *Fit to Be Tied*. Grand Rapids, Mich.: Zondervan, 1986.

Mow, Anna. *Your Child from Birth to Rebirth*. Grand Rapids, Mich.: Zondervan, 1963. (Carol's favorite.)

Smalley, Gary. *For Better or For Best*. Grand Rapids, Mich.: Zondervan, 1979. (For women.)

Smalley, Gary. *If Only He Knew*. Grand Rapids, Mich.: Zondervan, 1979. (For men.)

Smalley, Gary. *The Key to Your Child's Heart*. Dallas: Word, 1992.

Make Deposits in the Love Bank

**How can we make daily deposits of
loving communication in our children's lives?**

OCCASIONALLY WE GET A NOTICE FROM THE BANK notifying us that we have overdrawn our account. We have noticed that it always happens to us when something big is occurring, like going on vacation. One time as we walked out the door for our vacation, we grabbed the mail. We opened the notice from the bank and discovered an error of several thousand dollars. That led to total panic. All other activities came to a halt. Frantically we called the bank and then went over there for a personal visit. A big deposit had been recorded incorrectly. We worked through the process of fixing the problem. This problem distracted me (Carol) so much that when we finally resolved it and got into the car to leave for vacation, I left my wallet at the house. Having to do without the wallet reminded us of the problem during the entire vacation.

The lesson from the deficit: Don't overdraw your account. Even better, make enough deposits to ensure plenty of margin in the account. If we overdraw, then we not only have to make the extra effort to fix it, but sometimes we also have to live with the frustrating consequences it typically always causes.

Opening an Unconditional Love Account
Our children's lives parallel that bank account. They have a need for security and significance that come from unconditional love. When a deficit occurs in their lives, that threatens their security and significance, and then they panic. It's not hard to spot it when their account gets overdrawn.

- They seek attention.
- They want to control the situation.
- They get revenge (usually by clobbering a sibling!).
- They resist and rebel.
- They turn to their friends.
- They get depressed.

Only through communicating unconditional love can we make deposits in their account and get them out of a big deficit.

As we discussed in the last chapter, building intimacy with our children is a big investment in the relationship. In addition, we make another large investment when we communicate lovingly. Daily deposits of loving communication bring very positive results. Our children…

- have positive self-worth.
- have a willingness to obey.
- are less drawn to peer pressure.
- develop openness and honesty.
- set a pattern for healthy communication as they become more independent.

The most positive result, however, is that they will grasp God's love more easily because of the concrete example of love they have experienced. Many parents fall into the trap of expressing "if" love to their children. That means they love them if they perform properly. For example: "I love you *if* you get good grades." Other parents get trapped into expressing "because" love. For example: "I love you *because* you are beautiful/handsome." Sometimes we express that form of superficial love without even knowing it. Every time we do it, we undermine our children's sense of security and significance. Yet God desires for us to express "in spite of" love to our children. "I love you *in spite of* your attitude right now." That kind of love is totally unconditional. It comes from God to us, then through us to our children. It encourages our children's sense of security and significance. "In spite of" love from us prepares our children's hearts to receive God's love for them.

Communicating unconditional love to our children creates closeness and emotional warmth with them so that when we have to say "no" or discipline them, we can draw from a surplus in the account. As parents we are responsible to make the deposits that keep our children's accounts in the black until they learn for themselves how to let Jesus make deposits. Even then our children need consistent deposits of unconditional love from their parents.

Ross Campbell, child psychologist and author of *How to Really Love Your Teenager*, reinforces how critical communicating unconditional love really is by using the word picture of a gas tank instead of a bank account.

A teenager will strive for independence in typical adolescent ways–doing things by himself, going places without family, testing parental rules. But he will eventually run out of emotional gasoline and come back to the parent for conditional maintenance–for a refill. . . .

[**By communicating unconditional love we build reserves to draw from later.**]

During times when a teenager is striving for independence he may upset his parents to such an extent that the parent overreacts emotionally, and usually with excessive anger. This emotional overreaction, if too excessive or frequent, make it extremely difficult, and perhaps impossible, for the teenager to return to his parents for emotional refills. Then if parent-child communication is broken, a teenager may turn to his peers for emotional nurture. What a dangerous and frequently disastrous situation this is! [Ross Campbell, *How to Really Love Your Teenager*, Chariot Victor Publishing, 1981, p. 27, 30]

The principle remains the same using either illustration. By communicating unconditional love we build reserves to draw from later.

Avoiding Unnecessary Withdrawals

Before any of us opens a bank account, the bank personnel offer clear instructions on how to avoid overdrawing the account. We need that same instruction concerning loving communication with our children. Poor communication causes unnecessary withdrawals. Over time the relationship becomes depleted, resulting in an overdrawn account.

That's what happened to Amy (not her real name). Amy's parents brought her to talk to us. In the first thirty seconds we established the fact that she was unhappy. She had quit trying at school. Once an honor student, she was flunking all of her courses. Tension had mounted at home. Disrespect, dishonesty, and disobedience were everyday occurrences. Eventually she ran away from home with a boy. Why? What happened that brought this relationship to such a desperate point?

The problem had begun two years earlier when her parents relocated the family without communicating with her or considering her feelings. That began a pattern of poor communication that became increasingly worse. When she rebelled, her dad came down hard on her. He made her quit seeing her best friend across the street. He constantly criticized her rock music. When he got fed up, he put her on a three-year phone restriction. (That's three lifetimes to a teenager!) Once he yelled at her and threw her against the door. Her mom criticized Amy's friends, what she listened to on the radio, and what she wore. One day her mom opened a letter from Amy's boyfriend and read it.

In spite of all of this, Amy's parents desperately loved their daughter and wanted to break through to her. But they were going about it the wrong way. They had set up patterns of communication that expressed anything but unconditional love. When they came to see us, the parents had made so many unnecessary withdrawals that the account had not only been depleted but also was operating in the red.

Amy, on the other hand, had her own set of problems, most of them related to adolescence, and yet her struggles were no different than what most teenagers face.

1. They search for *identity* and *self-esteem*. They need people to respect them as individuals. Their request is simple: "Give me the chance to be me and not somebody else."
2. They react against parents' use of *authority* and *discipline*.

They need space to express their newfound independence. They beg us: "Trust me and treat me like an adult, not like a little kid."

3. They have an almost desperate frustration over the *failure to communicate*. They need for us to open the lines of communication and keep them open, even when they seem to do everything in their power to shut them down. Their heartfelt desire: "Please listen to me and not just talk at me." [Adapted from Fritz Ridenour, *What Teenagers Wish Their Parents Knew about Kids*, Word, 1982, p. 13.]

Amy and her family struggled with all three of these issues. Sadly their poor communication kept the door locked on the other two.

What happens to children when they become adolescents is like going from an open field into a dark cave. Teenagers "go into the cave" by withdrawing inside themselves and pulling their thoughts and feelings in after them. For example, when our friend Rick [not his real name] went into the cave during adolescence, his easy-going, talkative demeanor with his friends disappeared at home. He refused to let his parents into the cave to find him. Because he hid in the cave most of the time at home, his side of the conversation sounded like: "Ugh." "Yep." "Hmm." "Wha."

Adolescents go into that cave for many reasons, but almost all of those reasons can be traced back to broken communication with their parents. Repeatedly we have heard teenagers make these statements to their parents.

"You don't understand me." They don't think their parents know where they are coming from, and if their parents did know, they are so out of it they couldn't relate anyway. It's the "my dad was a teenager in the Fred Flintstone era" routine. They say things like: "If my parents knew this, they would kill me. I could never tell them."

"You embarrass me." They know that we are going to say

MAKE DEPOSITS IN THE LOVE BANK   113

or do something stupid around their friends. One kid's mom let him out at school, where all of his friends were standing and yelled, "When you get home from school, you better pick up your underwear!" Now that is embarrassing!

"You don't pay attention to me." Often our children feel as if we shut them out. They try to talk to us, and we are preoccupied with the computer, our cell phone, TV, the newspaper, or some project we think is more important than they are. Because we don't pay attention, they don't open up to us.

"You put me down." The messages our children tend to internalize are the negative ones. All some kids hear is "Don't be such a jerk" or "You never do anything right." The constant flow of condemning statements, including teasing and sarcasm, hurts kids and makes them clam up. Not only do they feel the stinging criticism, but often they think we hate them.

> Teenagers "go into the cave" by withdrawing themselves and pulling their thoughts and feelings in after them.

"You won't let me grow up." During adolescence our children want to become independent. When they tell us to "buzz off," we tend to either cling more tightly or to withdraw. The balance of knowing when to let go and when to hold on is a delicate one.

In the midst of communication problems with our children, we need to learn to lovingly talk and listen without being defensive. If we can teach our children to do the same, we will have the basic tools to keep them out of the cave or to help bring them out if they are already in.

Using the Checkbook

Before making deposits in our bank account, we need to know how the checkbook works. In our relationship with our children, unconditional love is our asset in the bank and our communication skills are the checkbook. These skills create a channel through which our love can flow. Our communications checkbook allows us to dispense love, acceptance, affirmation, physical warmth, and availability. In order to do that we must be aware of our need to move from superficial levels of communication to deeper ones.

Communication experts point out five levels of communication that can move us from surface responses to intimate sharing.

1. *Clichés.* "How are you?"
2. *Facts.* "What did you eat for lunch?"
3. *Ideas.* "What do you think about that?"
4. *Feelings.* "How do you feel when that happens?"
5. *Intimate sharing.* "What is on your heart about that?" This level of conversation occurs only in those few relationships in which a person can open his or her heart and share deeply.

Some people find it easier than others to move from one level to another level. But if we want to communicate deeply into our children's lives, then we must make significant love deposits to reach the level of most intimate sharing. All families progress to the first three levels. Others may move to Level 4. But only families surrounded by unconditional love enjoy the opportunity to reach Level 5.

If we have unconditional love for our children, then how do we communicate it to them? The communication skills that follow will help us do that more effectively. Based on Ephesians 4:22-32, they help us not only have a biblical basis for how we communicate but also give us practical advice as well.

Change our attitudes. The Apostle Paul challenges us "to be made new in the attitude of your mind" (vv. 22-24). To do that he says we must lay aside our old way of thinking and put on our new self, which is created to be like God. What we learned in chapters 1-4 reminds us how to do that. What's exciting is that when we deal with our children in less than ideal circumstances, we can have the confidence that we have the attitudes and thoughts of Jesus. Before discussing issues with our children, we have found it wise to be alone for a few minutes, not to jot down an outline of what to tell them, but to focus on Jesus, asking to have the mind of Christ. Say something like this: "Jesus, I want to respond to my child in exactly the way you would respond." This tool, more than any other, sets the tone for the way our children will respond to us.

Speak honestly. "Putting off falsehood and speaking truthfully" are what the Apostle Paul recommends (vv. 25-26). The reason this is so critical in the family is that our children don't respond to our fact-filled logic, but rather they respond to feelings. Just as importantly, they don't respond to well-crafted speeches, but rather they respond to our behavior. They know whether or not we are being honest. We must make a practice of always dealing with our children honestly. I (Barry) remember my mother's amazing ability to know what I had been doing. She would say something like "What were you doing at _____." And then I knew that she knew exactly where I had been and what I had been doing. I never have gotten the courage to ask her, "How did you know that? Do you have a spy network or were my jeans bugged?" None of us wants to be dishonest. We just slide on the truth if we think it will make us look bad or hurt other's feelings. A few verses earlier, the Apostle Paul said, "speak . . . the truth in love" (Eph. 4:15). In the context of genuine, unconditional love the truth may hurt, but it will not wound. Always communicate honestly with your children.

Express thoughts positively. The Apostle Paul encourages us to avoid "unwholesome talk" (v. 29). We easily fall into the habit of negative comments. It became so bad at one point in our family that every time one person said something negative, the person who heard it would yell out "NUB." When any of us got five NUBs, punishment followed. (NUB stands for "Not Up Building"). It took us a while, but we broke the habit. Even now, years later, if one of our kids says something negative, another will shout, "NUB!" During the "NUB" phase we discovered three clues to curb negative responses.

1. *Don't cut.* Sarcasm, cynicism, and especially teasing begin as funny comments, but turn into a downward spiral of hurtful, cutting remarks. Making cutting comments about others is a severe form of insecurity. We cut others down in order to build up ourselves.
2. *Don't judge.* Criticizing others for their behavior sets the one criticizing above everyone else as better. Judging others is a severe form of pride. As one person said, "God created only one universe and only one Messiah to rule it. And you are not him!" All of us fall into that trap. The value of family is that it helps us resign as ruler of the universe.
3. *Don't threaten.* One student told his parents, "I am sick of your rules. I am going to join the Marines." He didn't quite have a grip on reality, but it was a threat. Threats set up an "us versus them" situation. We are family. We always want to be on the same side.

We need to have our family focus on making only comments that "build . . . others up according to their needs" (Eph. 4:29). These positive comments "benefit" the family. To offset the NUBs, the person who made the negative remark had to replace it with a positive one (an "UB," if you please). As you might imagine, this was sometimes strained and painful, but we all got the point.

Also during this time we learned three clues to encourage positive responses.

1. *Choose words carefully.* Instead of blurting out whatever comes to mind when we get frustrated, we need to think about the right words to say. When anyone in our family

"blurts," we say, "Let's go back and try that again." In time our children learned to move from "Dad, you're bugging me!" to "Dad, this is beginning to bother me a little. When you do that with my friends, it embarrasses me. Would you not do that?"

2. *Control the tone of voice.* The tone of voice can communicate a wide range of emotions. For example, if someone says, "Great," what does that mean? By the tone of voice it can communicate discouragement, anger, nonchalance, or enthusiasm. Choose the tone that will express the emotion you want to communicate.

3. *Choose the right time.* In their youthful enthusiasm kids always want to talk about it NOW or NEVER. To learn to communicate positively, we need to teach them through our example how to pick the appropriate time to talk about an issue. We can teach them to say, "Mom, I know you are busy now. Could you tell me when we could talk about something that is on my mind?" Yet from our side we need to be quick to drop what we are doing in order to give our children the focused attention they need RIGHT NOW.

One final note on speaking positively, especially to dads: It is OK to say "yes" to our kids. I find so many dads who respond with "I don't care what you say. The answer is no!" They could just as easily have said "yes" without jeopardizing anything. We need to say "yes" to our family every time we can.

Listen actively. Nothing frustrates children more than parents who don't listen. A predictable grunt, a pat answer, or an inattentive response causes our kids to want to yell at us, "You are not listening!" To get rid of that accusation and to improve our listening skills, use the "Stop! Look! Listen!" method.

STOP what you are doing immediately.
LOOK the other person in the eye.
LISTEN with both ears from the edge of your seat.

Once our children have our total attention, then we can complete the loop of the conversation by asking questions that clarify and keep the conversation moving.

"That's interesting. Tell me more."

"I'm interested in your point of view. Explain it to me."

"That seems like something really important to you. Tell me why."

> [
> **We need to say**
> **"yes" to our**
> **family every**
> **time we can.**
>]

As the conversation moves along, try to identify feelings and problems that go deeper than the surface conversation. Our children need us to help them identify their feelings and then verbally express them.

When our son came in and said, "Girls are weird. I'm never going to date again," it didn't take a psychiatrist to figure out that he had some strong feelings. We could have made one of several knee-jerk reactions (and we have in other conversations):

"I agree. Girls are weird, especially that one. I'm glad you're not going out with her again."

"Son, I don't want to hear you talk about girls that way."

"Sit down over here and tell me every detail."

In order to listen actively, complete the conversation loop. Move to Level 4 or 5 communication. To do that, we said, "It sounds like you and Sara [not her real name] had a frustrating evening." Maybe at that point he will talk about it. Since he did not, we asked, "Do you want to talk about it?" He did. We tried to listen for his feelings. Then we gave him some feedback that didn't pass judgment on him or the girl but empathized with his feelings. We let him know that we understood his feelings. We discovered that he felt as if he didn't understand girls and that one had hurt him previously. We tried not to offer advice, to overanalyze the situation, or to ask too many questions. Once he got it all out, then we offered some suggestions to help him think through his feelings.

This kind of active listening unravels the threads of anger, frustration, and hurt, and it gets to the heart of an issue.

Avoid conversation stoppers. Offering another practical way to communicate, the Apostle Paul wrote, "Do not grieve the Holy Spirit of God" (Eph. 4:30), and then he followed that with the kinds of things that grieve the Holy Spirit: "bitterness, rage and anger, brawling and slander, along with every form of malice" (v. 31). All of these relate to the kinds of negative emotions that can lurk behind a conversation. Those emotions can destroy communication and a relationship.

A fourteen-year-old daughter dashes in and announces emphatically, "I'm not going camping with the family this weekend because I want to go to a party. I'm going to stay with a friend." When the mother hears this, if she is struggling with any of the negative emotions mentioned above, then she will yell back something like this: "Oh, no, you're not, 'Miss Priss.' You always think you can have your way. Well, you can't. The answer is no, and that's final. I'm not talking about it anymore." The daughter storms to her room and slams the door. The door was slammed on communication as well. Out of the list of "conversation stoppers" below and on the next page, how many did the mother use in the above conversation?

- preaching
- nagging
- threatening
- ridiculing
- breaking a confidence
- withdrawing into silence
- using sarcasm
- name calling
- discouraging

- commanding
- responding defensively
- not thinking before speaking
- bringing up the past
- attacking

In that brief conversation, the mother used all but breaking a confidence. She condemned her child and reflected her own negative emotions, revealing that her own needs were not being met. These responses communicate volumes to her daughter, who then cuts off all further meaningful conversation.

All of us get trapped into these emotions sometimes. As we listen to our conversations with our children and hear these negative responses coming out, let's ask ourselves what emotion is at the root of them and then ask the Holy Spirit to remove the negative responses.

Respond kindly. The final instruction that the Apostle Paul gives us in Ephesians 4 is to respond with kindness, compassion, and forgiveness to those around us (v. 32). When those three characteristics drive our conversations, we will respond to all people, and especially our children, with the spirit of Jesus Christ. Often we make a harsh response when *kindness is* what is needed. Frequently emotions run high, causing everyone to lose perspective when what is needed is the *compassion* of Jesus to focus us on His love. Many times we say and do things that hurt others, which calls for asking *forgiveness*. Without these three qualities to guide our conversations, we easily get confused about how to respond, especially when the conversation is not pleasant. But with these qualities we can ask questions, offer advice, listen with a sympathetic ear, and assert our viewpoint when necessary, so that we respond lovingly to a volatile child.

We have found that when we adhere to the following guidelines, we have been able to express kindness, compassion, and forgiveness to our children.

1. Never argue with a child's feelings.
2. Don't be threatened by a child's ambivalent attitudes or strong feelings.
3. Discern the difference between accepting a person and approving his or her behavior.
4. Always communicate respect.
5. Reply sensitively to sensitive subjects.
6. Make family decisions with the entire family.
7. Overlook irritating and unfavorable behavior when your children are tired or under stress.
8. Say no only when that is the best and only response; then stick by it.
9. Ask forgiveness as often as necessary.
10. Keep talking since silence solves nothing.

Mastering these communication skills deepens our awareness of our children and our sensitivity to their needs. Then we will not only understand their heart feelings, but we will bond with them at the deepest level.

Making Profitable Deposits

Avoiding unnecessary withdrawals and mastering communication skills certainly make a difference in the investment we make in our children. But, truthfully, those prove to be totally inadequate unless we spend the necessary time with our children. Only when time spent becomes a daily reality in our homes, can we have the confidence that our children will grow up with a passion for God.

Moses instructed parents on *what* to teach our children.

> Hear, O Israel: The Lord our God, the Lord is one. Love the Lord your God with all your heart and with all your soul and with all your strength. These commandments that I give you today are to be upon your hearts. Impress them on your children. (Deut. 6:4-7)

Then he gave clear direction on when to teach our children.

> Talk about them when you sit at home and
> when you walk along the road, when you lie
> down and when you get up. (Deut. 6:7)

Think about it: When else is there?

Since the average father spends less than thirty-eight seconds a day in direct contact with his children, we need to develop the habit of spending *both* quality and quantity time with them. If we go into a steak house and order a big juicy sirloin, we will not be very happy if the waitress brings out a big plate with only a one-ounce steak on it and announces, "We specialize in quality, not quantity." [James Dobson, "Focus on the Family" video series]

Why should our children feel any less disappointment when we don't spend quantity time communicating with them? Every time we get with them and loving communication occurs, we make deposits that will generate large interest payments in the future.

Ginny, our eleven year old, wrote this note on our last trip to the beach:

> I've always enjoyed being
> with my mommy after school
> when she picks me up and
> takes me to get something to
> eat, and on Wednesdays we
> go to piano. I've always loved
> being with her.

[**The average father spends less than thirty-eight seconds a day in direct contact with his children.**]

That time investment has paid off with our other children, and it will pay off for Ginny. And it will pay off for every child whose parents implement this "when else is there?" strategy in practical ways.

"When you sit at home…"

With kids going in several directions, seemingly at once, making the time to sit down together is hard work. We have found it necessary to make specific daily and long-term plans to spend time together.

We use mealtimes to talk. Plan carefully for those mealtimes when all of the family will be together. Prepare a good meal. Turn off the TV. Take the phone off the hook. Begin the meal with a blessing. After the food goes around the table, ask each person to talk about what happened during the day. Begin with a different person each time so the talkers don't dominate. As each one talks, ask lots of questions. This keeps the conversation going, and soon everyone gets into the action by talking to each other. This Level 2 conversation helps us as parents stay informed on what's going on in our kids' lives. Meanwhile, our children will build relational and communication skills including manners, listening, and sensitivity to others.

Sitting around the table, we can initiate Level 3 conversation by asking thought-provoking questions: "What did you think about _____ on the news tonight?" "How do you think we can act on what the pastor said in his sermon today?" Your children's observations will give you keen insight into what they think.

After dinner play *The Ungame* (available at most Christian bookstores). Designed to stimulate conversation, it will quickly move the family to Level 4 conversation. Keep some of the questions from the game in a basket near the table. If *The Ungame* is unavailable, make up questions. Use these for starters:

- Tell about a time when you felt proud of yourself.
- If you could change your age, what age would you rather be? Why?
- If you became President of the United States, what two

things would you do first?

- How do you look when you get angry? Why do you think you look that way?

Questions like these initiate personal sharing that reveals thoughts and feelings.

"When you walk along the road…"

We have a lake in our neighborhood. In the twenty-seven years we have lived here, we have walked to and around that lake thousands of times. It's our way of taking a few unhurried minutes as a couple or with our children. Just walking along encourages conversation.

Yet since most of us don't walk as much as people did in ancient civilizations, driving in the car provides prime time for conversation. Not only can we use it to catch up on the "day-to-day stuff," but because we have our children's undivided attention, we can also move into deeper levels of conversation. In high school Scott had to leave at 7 A.M. to drive twenty-five minutes to get to school. Before he got his driver's license, we drove him. What an opportunity to talk! We heard about the pressures of tests, the frustrations of sports injuries, or the excitement of a weekend outing with his friends. We had some serious talks about the girl scene on those trips as well. We prayed every day, memorized verses, and talked about the Lord. We tried to max out this time by planning some of the converation topics, but mostly we tried to make it his time.

For people who travel, taking our kids on a trip scores big with them. Usually we take them one at a time, but not always. We took Scott on a trip to North Carolina and saw the last game UNC played before moving into the Dean Dome. Katie went with Carol and Carol's mother to a weekend women's retreat, where all three spoke to the ladies. That only deepened the already close bond between the three generations of women in our family. Jonathan flew with Carol when he was about ten. With his siblings, Jonathan was quiet. Mostly he grinned and listened to everyone else. Yet the minute he sat down on the plane, he started talking and didn't stop until the plane landed. Carol listened in amazement. It was as if someone had let him out of the box and turned on his switch. Ginny, eleven, and Barry recently returned from Baton Rouge, Louisiana. They stayed with friends, toured the capitol and the LSU campus, and ate out several times. Ginny got the Princess bear Beanie Baby as a gift. Throw in Barry speaking three times, and it was quite a weekend. We had plenty to talk about for weeks after that.

One of the most significant communication times with our children has been their "preteen trip" when they were eleven. For example, Barry and Scott went camping.

> The first night we set up our camp and cooked "silver turtles." The next day we hiked up Blood Mountain on the Appalachian Trail. After a long, hard climb, we arrived at the top exhausted. We lay on a big rock, ate and drank our snacks, and talked as we took in the breathtaking view. Later that day we found a "swimming hole," a freezing, fast-moving stream. Each time we went across, we tried to beat our record for how far we got swept downstream.

Carol and Katie opted for a cozy mountain cabin with a fireplace.

> We worked so hard to get a good fire going. We laughed and laughed because it wouldn't start. We enjoyed visiting Babyland General, the home of the Cabbage Patch dolls. We shopped in a quaint village, visited a friend, and ate in a cozy restaurant on a rainy night.

On these trips with all of our children, we took along James Dobson's tapes *Preparing for Adolescence.* We listened to some of the tapes in the car as we drove to our destination. We listened to others throughout the weekend. After the first tape on self-esteem, Barry asked Scott what he did and did not like about himself. Scott said, "There's nothing I don't like about me. I like everything." That was the end of that conversation! The others viewed themselves a little more realistically. Those weekends opened the door to many conversations about love, sex, and dating over the next few years.

"When you lie down..."

From birth we have made putting our children to bed a big deal. When Ginny, our youngest by eight years, was a toddler, she loved nothing better than to prop up on the pillows with a pile of books, snuggled next to Mom, Dad, or one of her siblings. We read, played, and talked about Jesus. When we prayed, she covered her face with her hands and mumbled. Now years later, when we put her to bed, she has five pillows, books all around, and prays the sweetest prayers.

When Ginny came along, the older children began to relive their days of bedtime when they were her age. They shuffled through their old books to pick out some of their old favorites for their little sister. They even came to Carol, got into bed with her, and wanted her to read the old Dr. Seuss and Berenstein Bears books to them. We were reminded that those times of communication had made significant deposits in their emotional accounts.

For the older children bedtime helps them unwind and talk about the issues of their day. Sometimes feelings come out that neither they, nor we, were aware of. Some days our children act irritable and picky. (Some days so do we.) When we ask them what's wrong, usually they don't know what to say. They may not even know why they are feeling as they do. On such nights we lie down beside that child and try to talk it through. If nothing else, our physical presence reassures them. A good back rub adds a touch that says, "I love you." On one such occasion Katie burst into tears, pouring her heart out about the hurt underneath her surface irritability. A time of prayer naturally follows, confessing any sin and asking the Lord to heal the hurt.

In our children's earlier years we used a back rub called "The Garden" to spur conversation. We began by "digging" out all of the hard soil and rocks–a vigorous rubbing of the back coinciding with confessions of the day (a fight with a sibling, a negative attitude). Then we "planted" rows of seed. These orderly pokes on the back created giggling while the child listed what he needed to plant (patience with a sibling, a positive attitude). Then finger movements representing the gentle rain and the warm sun soothed them off to sleep. "The Garden" provided a creative approach to talking and praying.

As our children moved into adolescence, they thought they had outgrown those "tuck in" times. During Scott's early adolescence, he announced one night, "I can tuck myself in, I can say my own prayers, and I can kiss myself goodnight." It became a standing joke to see if Scott could get to bed, "tuck himself in," and go to sleep before we could get into his room. We playfully persisted. Barry would attack, taking a running leap at the bed. Then a wrestling match ensued. After wrestling and laughing, we offered up a brief prayer.

If you can stay awake, the time after your teenager's date or other activity can provide "when you lie down" talk time. When our kids came in, we asked a simple question, "How was it?" That opened the door. They would tell us about what they had done. If something bugged them, they probably wouldn't blurt it out, but most likely it would slide into the conversation somewhere. Sometimes they desired privacy. We tried to honor that. As we identify their feelings and talk with them about those feelings, we make big deposits in the relationship account.

"When you get up…"

One child pops out of bed ready to attack the day.

Another drags himself out of bed, one toe at a time, and then wants to eat breakfast with his head in the plate of eggs. With those two extremes and some kids in between, how can we communicate effectively when they arise, especially if we parents are not "morning persons"?

Our family struggles to find the balance. We try to establish some sense of continuity in our morning routine because of the value of that communication time for our whole family. We know that breakfast provides a time when all of us regularly touch base. We find out what each person faces for the day. We coordinate schedules. We share a verse or thought from the Bible. We pray for God's blessing and guidance on the day. In spite of the wildness and the crazy laughing (even during the prayers sometimes), that brief time draws us together. Even with all of the effort it takes, our morning time communicates that we won't face anything that day that God and our family can't handle together.

Now that two of our children are happily married and the others are getting older, we can see the value of time spent, focused attention, physical touch, and a constant awareness of the presence of God. The investment we made in their accounts has paid a bigger dividend than we could have ever imagined. Our hope and prayer is that it will be so with your family as well.

Taking Action

Ask a friend to give you honest feedback on how you communicate with your children. Then take that information and make a list of three ways you will improve loving communication with your children. Choose one from that list to do this week, building it into a specific activity that will require time and attention given to your child.

Penetrating Questions

1. Looking at the indicators of an overdrawn account on page 108, is your account overdrawn with your child?

2. From the results of deposits of loving communication listed on page 109, would you say you are making the kind of deposits needed for your child to know he or she is unconditionally loved?

3. Has your child made any of the statements on page 112 and 113 that indicates he or she has gone into "the cave"?

4. If your teenager is in "the cave" or if your child could be there some day, what do you need to do now to get him or her out, or keep him or her from going in?

5. Which checks do you have in your communications checkbook currently? Which ones do you need to add?

6. What changes do you need to make in your schedule to have quantity time with your child?

7. What aggressive plan do you have in mind to make profitable deposits according to the outline in Deuteronomy 11:19?

8. Does your spouse think you have a realistic picture of your account? Courageously ask.

Fresh Ideas
• Do an "Investment Analysis" by reviewing last week's withdrawals and deposits with your child. To determine the activity in your account, list all of the negative communication you had with your child in one column and mark it "Withdrawals." Then list all of the positive communication in a column marked "Deposits." Figure out your "balance" by subtracting withdrawals from deposits.

• To stop the withdrawals, analyze where your conversations got off track and why.

- Using your communications checkbook, write down one phrase regarding what you will do to:
  —Change your attitude.
  —Speak honestly.
  —Express thoughts positively.
  —Listen actively.
  —Avoid conversation stoppers.
  —Respond kindly.

- Use the guidelines from Deuteronomy 11:19 to devise a plan for making positive daily deposits for your child.

- Make a large deposit by planning a special one-on-one time with your child this week. Think of an activity that he or she would like to do and then do it.

Further Reading
Bell, Valerie. *Getting Out of Your Kids' Faces and Into Their Hearts.* Grand Rapids, Mich.: Zondervan, 1994.

Campbell, Ross. *How to Really Love Your Child.* Colorado Springs: Chariot Victor Publishing, 1977.

Campbell, Ross. *How to Really Love Your Teenager.* Colorado Springs: Chariot Victor Publishing, 1981.

Mow, Anna B. *Your Child from Birth to Rebirth.* Grand Rapids, Mich.: Zondervan, 1963. (Carol's favorite.)

Wikinson, Bruce. *Family Walk.* Atlanta: Walk Through the Bible.

Set "Speed Limits" that Lead to Independence

**How do we discipline our children so that
they move from dependence to independence?**

"THE GREAT LATE NIGHT TOMATO FIGHT." At fourteen
years old, our son Scott was about to attend this annual
church youth event for the first time. The older guys battled
the younger ones to see who could smash each other with

the most tomatoes. The purpose and redeeming value of this event is yet to be determined. Scott, however, took this event seriously. He dressed in dark clothes and used charcoal to blacken his face. He went with the high school guys to plan strategy. Then they drove in a pickup to the farmer's market to get extra tomatoes they needed.

Carol and I had been out for the evening. The call was waiting when we arrived home. As parents there are two calls we never want to receive: (1) "Your child has been in an accident." (2) "Your child is under arrest." The officer said to me, "Your son has been arrested." Shocked, we asked, "What for?" He replied, "Stealing property." "There must be some mistake," we replied. "Is your son's name Scott St. Clair?" he asked. Again we said, "Surely some mistake…" He cut in, "Is your son's name…" We got the idea.

When we arrived at the police station, our son's criminal activity unfolded. Earlier, after Scott and his friends arrived at the farmer's market to pick up the tomatoes, half of them went into the store and half of them stayed out. The ones waiting in the truck continued to talk through their strategy. They wanted to build a barricade so the older guys could not get to them. As they talked, they saw a big, old crate in the trash pit. Ah-ha—the perfect barricade! They got it and put it into the truck. At this point five security officers came to arrest them. They took them to the security office, charged them with stealing, took their pictures, fingerprinted them, tape-recorded their confession, and called their parents.

They had one frightened fourteen year old! When we got home, he told us the entire story. He said when they took his picture, he knew he was going to jail. He saw his entire future going down the drain. The next day we went back over to the farmer's market and got it all straightened out. Clearly the security officers were overzealous. Yet Scott and his friends should not have taken the crate without asking. And his parents should have had more control in that situation.

Blindsided by the situation (after all, it was a church

event!), we had not set the limits needed to care for our son properly. As children get older, especially when they enter adolescence and then get their driver's license, setting boundaries becomes more and more of an issue. From early on, the basic question we parents need to answer is: "How can we discipline our children so they become self-disciplined?"

The Perfect Picture

Having the following vivid picture in our minds will help us set the stage for answering that question. We have all watched baby birds with their mouths wide open, turned upward, and waiting for their mother to feed them. We say, "Oh, how cute." And it is. That is the picture when our children are younger. But as they get older and especially as they move into adolescence, the picture changes. The cute little birds scramble up the side of the nest, and with their weak little legs and fragile bodies they try to jump out of the nest. That is a scene of intense danger. What if they jump and can't fly? The mother bird lets her babies jump and try to flap their wings. When they can't, the mother bird swoops down and grabs her babies with her strong claws just before they crash to the ground.

That picture clearly portrays our role in parenting our children as they grow older. When do we take away the limits and let them try things on their own? And when do we sense the intense danger and swoop down to rescue them by imposing limits on them? And how do we discipline them in a way that creates the desire for God's discipline in their lives?

Panic Mode

Lest we kid ourselves, we need to know that the dangers to our children are real. In one hour in the United States:

- 114 teens run away from home.
- 28 girls give birth to illegitimate children.
- 44 girls under nineteen will abort their babies.

- 1,370 teens will take some form of drugs.
- 376 teens will get drunk.
- 570 will experience the trauma of a broken home.
- 456 will be beaten, molested, or abused.
- 58 will attempt suicide.
- 1 will succeed at attempting suicide.

[Youth for Christ statistics]

[**The goal: To move our children from dependence to independence.**]

Parents intuitively know these statistics are true, and we are scared to death that our kids will become one of them. As a result we parent our children from a panic mode. In that mode we tend to swing the pendulum too far in one of two directions. In one direction we tend to be too permissive. Because we fear that our children will not like us, we try too hard to be their friend. In the other direction we tend to be too restrictive. We fear that our children will get involved with the wrong crowd and in negative activities. This becomes much more pronounced when our children reach adolescence. Either way, we panic, throwing away the lid of restriction or slamming it down on our children. Neither one of these fear responses will get us to our goal of creating a desire for God's discipline in our children's lives.

From Dependence to Independence

What is our goal when we discipline our children? The goal is to move our children from dependence to independence.

Sometimes our kids don't give us much encouragement that they will ever reach that goal. One of "the world's great theologians," Erma Bombeck, wrote this about her son.

For years I have been telling myself that my son does not do well in school because he is marching to a different drummer. Now I have the feeling if he doesn't shape up, he's going to goose step his way right into the unemployment office. The other morning he shuffled into the kitchen and said, "I will be glad when I can retire." "From what?" I asked. "From studying," he said. "Frankly," I grumbled, "your father and I are worried about you. The only thing you have passed all year is your eye examination." "They don't teach me what I want to be," he said. "I want to be a South American baseball catcher for Baltimore." The drums again. I heard them when he was 6. When he spent hours in the bathroom filling up his navel with water squeezed from a washcloth and announced at dinner, "It takes 14 drops to fill an average navel." I smiled to myself, "My son, the scientist." When he was 8 and took the wheels off my sweeper, attached them to the clothes hamper and wheeled it in to find his lucky socks on test days, I smiled knowingly, "My son, the engineer." At 9 he turned our bathroom into a sweating, teeming jungle for a horned toad that eventually bled through the eyes and died. And the drums chanted, "My son, the vet." At 14 when his boyfriends were taking girls [out], he stayed home and listened to his tape recording of belches recorded after a typical cafeteria lunch. Boom. Boom. My son, the creative producer.

Now I wasn't sure. "You'd better hustle," I said, "or you'll be late for school." "Do I have to go today?" he asked. " I read where a school in California gives you trading stamps if you show up for classes. Boy, would that be something!" "I guess it would be an incentive," I said. "Incentive, heck. You could save stamps till you got enough to redeem them for a car. Then you could blow." The drums. They were distinct and clear now. They said, "My son, the bum." [Erma Bombeck, "At Wit's End," *The Courier-Journal,* Louisville, Kentucky]

Many of us identify with that conversation. We have had similar ones that have gone unpublished. From those conversations we know it takes great wisdom to make the daily decisions that will move our children toward independence. We need to follow this general rule of thumb in making these decisions: control the rate of independence by matching it to the level of our child's maturity.

To get the big picture of how this works, look at the diagram.

[
Control the rate of independence by matching it to the level of our child's maturity.
]

From Dependence to Independence

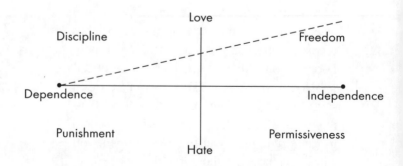

Punishment is not the parenting approach we want to take, because punishment implies a penalty imposed on an offender for a crime. When we parent from the punishment quadrant, it means that we emphasize the power of the authority, the consequences of the "crime," and the problem person—not the problem itself. For example, we might say, "I told you to come home on time. Since you didn't, you are grounded. Don't be so stupid next time." Treating our kids like criminals will cause them to become criminals.

Permissiveness does not serve us well either, because permissiveness allows children to do whatever they want, thus leading to a lack of control. When we parent from the permissiveness quadrant, it means that we emphasize a lack of authority, no consequences, and a lack of concern for the child involved. For example, we might say, "Look, I don't care. You can come home whenever you want. Whatever you do doesn't make any difference to me." Treating our children with such disrespect causes them to grow up with a lack of respect for themselves and other people as well, including their parents.

Many parents fall into the trap of these two approaches. When their child becomes a teenager, either they get scared and try to clamp down or they disengage from their child's life.

> **Discipline: external control that, when removed, leads to internal self-control.**

Discipline, on the other hand, moves us in a positive direction. We define discipline as *external control that, when removed, leads to internal self-control.*

Discipline is the *doorway* that leads to freedom. Utilizing discipline allows our children to fly out of the nest and soar, rather than crash into the side of the mountain.

We can grab hold of the knob of that door by understanding Hebrews 12:7-11. The writer explains it this way:

> Endure hardship as discipline; God is treating you as sons. For what son is not disciplined by his father? If you are not disciplined (and everyone undergoes discipline), then you are illegitimate children and not true sons. Moreover, we have all had human fathers who disciplined us and we respected them for it. How much more should we submit to the Father of our spirits and live! Our fathers disciplined us for a little while as they thought best; but God disciplines us for our good, that we may share in his holiness. No discipline seems pleasant at the time, but painful. Later on, however, it produces a harvest of righteousness and peace for those who have been trained by it.

From these verses several insights become clear.

- The Lord uses difficult circumstances to discipline us (v. 8).
- All fathers should discipline their children (v. 8).
- Without discipline we feel like "illegitimate children" (v. 8).
- Disciplining our children produces respect (v. 9).
- Discipline works only if we submit to our (Heavenly) Father (v. 9).
- God disciplines us for our good–to make us holy (v. 10)
- No discipline is pleasant (v. 10).
- Discipline results in a harvest of righteousness (that is, children who are rightly related to God therefore will think rightly and behave rightly; v. 11).
- Discipline results in peace (that is, harmony in your home now and your children's homes in the future; v. 11).
- These benefits come only to those who are trained in discipline (v. 11).

Discipline comes from the very heart of God. When we understand that the results of His discipline lead us to "a harvest of righteousness and peace" for our children, not only can we stand the "pain" of implementing it, but we can actually enter into it with great enthusiasm.

The following diagram summarizes the stark contrast among these three parenting approaches:

Contrast in Parenting Approaches

	Punishment	Discipline	Permissiveness
Purpose:	Punish wrong	Promote growth	Avoid punishment
Focus:	Past wrong action	Future correct attitude	No action
Parent's attitude:	Anger/hostility	Concern	Apathy
Resulting behavior:	Rebellion	Respect/obedience	Rebellion
Resulting emotion:	Fear/guilt	Security/love	Rejection

"You Decide"

Once we understand how discipline works and decide to follow God's approach to it, then we need to know how to make it work on a practical level. That's hard because parenting can get extremely tiring. When we get tired, discipline is the first to go. After that, chaos reigns.

One Christmas we received a holiday letter from our friends who had three children under two. The letter began: "Some 5,840 diapers ago we sat down to bring you holiday greetings." The letter continued: "A concerned friend actually asked, 'What do you do for fun?' So we made up a list.

- Make popcorn and read *What Do You Do with a Kangaroo?* for the umpteenth time while disentangling my urchins from yards of audiotape.
- Play flip the coin for who digs the new roll of toilet paper out of the toilet bowl this time.
- Deck the hall with boughs of holly while 16-month-old Abby decks Annie, and Ian decks the living room (for the fifth time) with fireplace soot.
- Play "Let's-drive-around-and-look-at-the-Christmas-lights-til-your-Daddy-gets-home-you-guys-are-ripping-up-the-joint."

If we are going to offer practical discipline to our children, then we need to stay on our toes as parents. We know that's no easy task! Rich Wilkerson wrote a book with a very illogical title: *Hold Me While You Let Me Go*. Yet that title summarizes our contradictory job as parents. Raising kids includes controlling them, restraining goofiness, preventing harm, running the show, and calling the shots. If we leave our children unsupervised for twenty minutes, they will kill each other. That is the *hold me* part.

On the other hand, we don't want to do this forever. Over an eighteen-year period we want to launch our kids into responsible independence. We want to get them to the place where they are self-controlled. That means we have to constantly adjust. Each child is a moving project learning new skills on almost a weekly basis. They become a little more competent each day. We have to stay on top of the situation or we will find ourselves sounding like a broken record: "No, you're not ready to do that yet!" That is *the while you let me go part*.

Dean Merrill further explains that our kids are going to grow up on us anyway. In fact, they had better. We certainly don't want them frozen in time, and one of the best ways to let them know that we understand this is to find safe settings in which to use two magic words: *You decide!* Those decisions can be low risk: Your child wants to pick out her own outfit, and it consists of plaids and stripes. Sometimes the decisions are medium risk: Your child wants to go out with someone you don't know. At other times the decision can be high risk: Your child wants to drink or take drugs. If a child is not allowed to make independent decisions until he or she leaves home, then when that child does make decisions, they are not likely to be good ones. Far better for your child to hear the words "you decide" from loving and wise parents along the way. [Dean Merrill, "You Decide," *Focus on the Family* magazine, October 1996, pp. 6-7]

Boundaries Needed
When we make a list of all of the areas where our children need boundaries, it can become rather overwhelming. We made this quick list, and certainly it is not exhaustive.

1. Eating
2. Safety
3. Chores
4. TV
5. Bedtime
6. Friends
7. Activities
8. Behavior
9. Studies
10. Phone
11. Transportation
12. Curfew
13. Dating
14. Sex
15. Family time

You can add to the list, or even better, reduce it to those one or two key issues your children face now. We have found that it doesn't do any good to focus on those issues before

[**Develop a specific plan for an area of discipline only when it becomes an issue.**]

they become real issues for our children. Besides, the goal is not to see how many rules we can have, but how few. To "develop a plan" ahead of time on each of those specific issues wastes time. Some of them will never be significant issues with some children. However, some of them will! When they do become issues, they come on with a vengeance. For that reason we need to have an overall approach to decide how we will handle the entire issue of setting limits. From that launchpad we can develop a specific plan for an area when it becomes an issue.

What guidelines can we use to set boundaries? When our children were younger, we made those decisions on a basis of biblical values and intuition. When Scott became a teenager, that simple and relaxed approach needed both more intensity and focus. We forged our guidelines in "the heat of the battle."

I (Barry) was lying on Scott's bed one night, as I did almost every night. He confided in me for the first time that he wanted to take a girl out. Having worked with teenagers for years, I knew this day would come sooner or later. I had hoped for later. He was fourteen. The girl was sixteen! Immediately I gave him all the standard arguments. "At fourteen you can go on group dates. At sixteen you can double date. At eighteen you can single date." After I said it, he laughed. In fact, he laughed so hard that he fell off the bed. I wasn't laughing, however. When I thought about it later, I realized that I had no basis for saying what I said except that is what I had heard other parents say. I knew I had some serious homework to do. I asked Scott to give me a couple of weeks to think about it. First, Carol and I set out to establish the general guidelines from which we would make these decisions. Then we addressed the dating dilemma.

We discovered the following general guidelines for how to set limits. They have served us well in raising all of our children from toddlerhood through their teenage years.

1. *Define it.* In defining what the guideline will be, we tried to answer two questions:
   - What is expected?
   - What happens if the boundary is crossed?

Norman Wright and Rex Johnson encourage us:

> Set your limits on behavior but not on opinions. This is perhaps the most difficult guideline for parents to carry out without becoming overly threatened. A free expression of opinion, with proper rules of courtesy, is one of the healthiest goals a family can work toward. [Norman Wright and Rex Johnson, *Building Positive Parent Teen Relationships*, Harvest House, 1977, p. 47]

2. *Give reasons for it.* Often parents don't give reasons when telling their children what they can and cannot do. Maybe you have had a conversation like this:

"Mom, can I go…"
"No!"
"Why not?"
"Because I said so! And besides, I'm your mother."
(Under his breath) "I thought I knew you from some place." (Out loud) "Everybody else is going!"
"If everybody else was jumping over the cliff, would you jump too?"
(Under his breath again) "With a mother like you, I am considering it."

Every rule deserves a reason. Our children need to know the principle and the practical reason so they can apply it. Teenagers, especially, question their parents' values and rules. They will relate better to practical ones that they can understand. Dr. Ross Campbell in the classic book *How to Really Love Your Teenager* explains it like this:

> One of the reasons so many teenagers turn against spiritual values is that they are given too many moralistic reasons for rules and/or restrictions. During these rebellious, defiant, possibly hostile periods, parents are wise to give practical reasons for their decisions. Once the reason is given, however, you certainly are not required to defend it like a doctoral thesis. Arguing with your teenager over the adequacy or legitimacy of the reason is seldom warranted. As long as the answer is reasonable, stating it simply is generally sufficient. Being willing to argue about it usually invites further disagreement and anger. [Ross Campbell, *How to Really Love Your Teenager,* Colorado Springs: Chariot Victor Publishing, 1981, p. 78]

[**Every rule deserves a reason.**]

Without offering reasons, we force our children to operate by extrinsic motivation (see Action #3). They may conform to the rule, but they have no intrinsic motivation to live by the principle behind the rule. Our objective is to encourage motivation by giving them a reason for the action we want them to take.

3. *Discuss it.* Agreeing with what Ross Campbell says above, how do we encourage discussion without getting into an

argument? We have found that setting aside a time to sit down and talk about it works wonders. This approach will not work when underlying tension and unresolved conflict linger under the surface. In that case, deal with that first. Talk about it honestly. Listen carefully. Ask forgiveness. And keep the relationship, not the issue, as your top priority.

If the situation is not resolved simply and if it appears to be or actually is more complex, then taking the following steps will put you in the positive situation of establishing the guideline and keeping communication open:

- Draw up a proposal.
- Talk through the proposal.
- Negotiate the proposal until you agree. (Parents always have the final say!)

Joseph and Lois Bird clarify how to handle that.

> The rule is you can state your opinions, your convictions, your likes and dislikes; we are willing to listen, consider the matter, and discuss it. We will not, however, enter into a prolonged debate leading nowhere. Once a decision is made–after consideration of what they have to present–that's it. [Joseph and Lois Bird, *Power to the Parents*, Doubleday, 1972, pp. 111-12]

Once you have had the initial conversation, set up a time to discuss it again for evaluation. Clear the path for your child to talk to you about the issue any time that is appropriate.

4. *Be on the same team with it.* Slant the conversation in such a way that your child knows that you are on the same

team. Instead of this issue becoming an "us versus them" situation, work toward making it a "we" situation. This diagram will give you a visual picture of the difference.

Creating a "same team" environment for discussion, whatever the issue, will move relationships with our children beyond survival into a special bond.

5. *Don't go overboard with it.* Instead of coming on like a military commander on the issue, approach your children in a way that will motivate them. Explain that your goal is to build discipline, values, and motivation in them, not to keep them from doing something they want to do. Show them the bigger picture: that you want them to become independent, and the only way to do that is with discipline.

Then when the issue has been discussed, we don't need to bring it up every time we see them or discuss it around others when our children are present.

6. *Be consistent with it.* We need to make our children responsible for carrying out the guideline. If our children move beyond the limit, then they will be responsible for the consequences. They will learn that there are positive consequences for positive behavior and negative consequences for negative behavior. Don't allow them to blame their lack of consistency on others. If they have a legitimate problem fulfilling their responsibility, then be understanding. Always go back to the agreement. That will keep you out of

the "I said/you said" syndrome. Taking away privileges is a good consequence when our children are younger. Grounding them for a reasonable amount of time is an excellent consequence when they are teenagers.

Back on the bed with my son Scott about two weeks later, I had thought through these guidelines and had "The Dating Agreement" in hand. We had our pillows propped up on the back of the bed sitting beside each other. I told him, "Scott, I've worked on this because I love you and because this is an important issue. I want to go all the way through this together. Then we can go back and discuss each point. Will that work for you?" He agreed. This is what I gave him.

The Dating Agreement

1. I can have one date per week on either Friday or Saturday except on special occasions. Church youth group meetings and church group activities are not considered dates.

2. I will date only committed Christian girls.

3. I will date properly by calling the girl in plenty of time and inviting her to a specific place at a specific time.

4. I will be allowed to stay out until 11 P.M. If I am running late for any reason, I will call home. If I am late without cause, my curfew time will move back one-half hour for the next week.

5. I will discuss each date with my parents beforehand, giving them all of the details. (Where I am going, when I will return, whom I will be with, and what the purpose of the occasion is.)

6. If my parents don't know the girl very well, I will have my first date at home with them. My parents will determine that.

7. I will limit where I go on my dates. All parties will have adult chaperones. Rock concerts and private dances will not be allowed, but school-sponsored functions are acceptable. All movies will be selected upon my parents' approval and the guideline of Philippians 4:8.

8. If my date and I want to talk at the end of a date, we will do so either with the group or in the girl's living room. We will not remain in the car.

9. I will be able to double date when I complete the following project and go over it with my parents: Study all of the Scriptures on pages 150-52 of *Dating: Going Out in Style* and write a brief paragraph on each one. I will select the five most important ones to me and write a specific paragraph on each one.

10. I will determine what holding hands and kissing mean to me. I will determine when I will hold hands or kiss a girl. I will go over that with my parents.

Some are reading this saying, "That is the most liberal document on dating I have ever read!" Others will respond, "I can't believe he asked his son to do those things. My child would never do that!" Either way it's OK because that was "our" dating agreement, not yours. You need to come up with one that meets your needs.

Interestingly, Scott agreed to every one of these points, except (can you guess?) number six. Many positive results came out of this exercise. Obviously we had established our guidelines. But also we avoided the superficial "You can date when you are 16" argument through setting up a project that allowed him to prove he was mature enough to date by completing it. Over the years of high school we followed this agreement. On several occasions we disagreed on a dating issue. "Let's go look at the agreement." We did. Several times I was wrong! Scott loved that. The agreement gave us something concrete to turn to. During those years we updated the agreement to fit his age and maturity. For example, we adjusted the curfew times. By the time he was a senior he had proved himself so faithful and responsible that his last year at home, he had no guidelines. We knew we could totally trust him to make wise decisions.

We had come a long way from "The Great Late Night Tomato Fight." Scott had moved from dependence to independence, and we felt confident that he was ready for Duke University. And he proved that he was. And your children will too.

Taking Action

Determine the one area where discipline is needed with your child, and then design a plan to address that issue from what you have learned in this chapter. First, write down your general approach to discipline, and then draw up a proposal to discuss with your child. Talk through it, and then negotiate it with your child.

Penetrating Questions

1. How would you describe your style of handling your children now (punishment, permissive, or discipline)?
2. In conversation with your spouse, how do you need to adjust or change your style?

3. Do you make disciplining decisions out of fear? If so,

how does that come across to your child? (Ask your spouse.)

4. What is the one discipline issue that is "hot" in your family right now?

5. What is your plan to address that issue according to what you have learned in this chapter?

6. What is your stated, long-range goal for disciplining your child? (Picture the mother bird). Are you holding your child with an open hand, desiring to move him or her to independence?

7. When you discipline your child, do you pray about what to do first? Do you communicate the reasons why? Do you express love in the discipline?

Fresh Ideas

1. Work on building the relationship before you discipline. Constantly show your child how much you love him or her. Set up a "date" on your schedule with your child each week. Let him or her pick what you do. Think through some good questions and topics to discuss.

2. When your child does something wrong, ask lots of questions to get to the real issue before passing judgment.

3. Write down all the rules your family has now and see how many you can eliminate.

4. Think of several "low risk" decisions that you are now making for your child and turn the decision-making process over to him or her. If your children are younger, design it as a game called "You Decide."

5. Take an issue you think your child is struggling with and practice writing up a "mock proposal" just to try your hand at it.

6. Join a group of parents at your church who have children the age of yours. Spend several sessions hammering out how you will discipline your children.

7. Determine your family's six core values with your spouse. Make that the basis for your guidelines and rules.

Further Reading

Campbell, Ross *How to Really Love Your Teenager*. Colorado Springs: Chariot Victor Publishing, 1981.

Dobson, James. *Dare to Discipline*, revised edition. Wheaton, Ill.: Tyndale House, 1996.

McDowell, Josh. *Right from Wrong*, Dallas: Word. 1994.

Discover a Sense of Destiny

How can our children find their unique destiny so they reach their maximum potential?

LLOYD'S OF LONDON followed 100,000 paper clips and observed that only about 2,000 were used to hold papers together. The bank said 14,163 clips were bent and twisted during telephone conversations. Another 19,143 were used as chips in card games. Another 7,200 clipped together garments. Another 5,434 became toothpicks or ear scratchers. Another 5,308 were converted into nail cleaners. Another 3,916 cleaned pipes. The rest fell ingloriously to the floor and were swept away.

How could something so neatly invented and so useful be so misused and often seemingly wasted? As parents we want to ask ourselves that question about our lives and the lives of our teenagers. Are we picking teeth and cleaning nails when God clearly has made our children and us for something much more?

When speaking to students, I (Barry) love to ask this question: "What is your dash?" They stare at me blankly. So I ask it again…and again. Then they ask the question: "What is your problem?" At that point I explain what "dash" means. In a cemetery most gravestones have a date when the person was born and a date when he or she died. In between those two dates is a dash. That dash represents what that person did with his or her life. "What is your dash?" is a great question!

When our children graduate from high school, one fourth of their lives is gone! During the next five years after that, they will make most of these life-changing decisions:

Graduating.
College.
Job.
Career.
Lifelong friends.
Marriage partner.

> When our children graduate from high school, one fourth of their lives is gone!

As a parent, that is a scary thought!

Our job is to help them determine their "dash" in their early years. When they pursue it, they will be well on their way to discovering God's destiny for their lives. They will determine their "dash" by answering life's three most important questions:

Who am I?
Where am I going?
How am I going to get there?

The first time I ever asked those questions, I had raised the window in my dorm room in college and was leaning out the window. I was trying to get some fresh air because everyone sleeping around me on the floor had gotten drunk the night before. That was the last straw for me.

Everything I did in high school had turned to gold. I had no reason to ask those hard questions while my life was consumed with being president of the student body, all-state basketball player, good student, dating any girl I chose, and going to college on a basketball scholarship.

After I arrived at college, however, all of the things that had success written on them in high school turned to failure. Now I was just a lowly freshman no different than anyone else. My first week of basketball I discovered that the guys 6'11", 6'12", and 6'13" were much bigger and better than I was! I made a 74 on my first history test–my major. Not good, especially because I could not brown-nose the teacher anymore. So I studied harder, and I made a 47 the next time! The girl I had invited for this particular weekend had called the day before and given me the shaft. If that wasn't enough, my grandmother, who was my closest friend in high school, had died just before school started. That morning as I opened the window for fresh air, the results of those disappointments flooded my mind, and I asked myself for the first time:

Who am I?
Where am I going?
How am I going to get there?

I had no answers, and it took me a year to discover the only answer: a relationship with Jesus Christ. Then it took me twenty more years to find many of the specific answers to related questions. That is why I took another year of my "dash" to put my insights in book form for students and parents saving them, I hope, years of time in discovering their own "dash." (Those books are entitled *Life Happens: Get*

Ready and *Life Happens: Help Your Teenager Get Ready*.)

What we want to see is the "big picture" on how to guide our children to discover their destiny by answering the three critical questions.

Who Am I?

This is the *destiny* question. Our struggle with how we answer the "Who am I?" question is illustrated in this story.

> The vehicles took us to the end of the road in the Maine woods. The counselors took the canoes off the racks and put three junior high kids under each one instructing them to carry the canoes to the water. Three scrawny guys, who already had backpacks and supplies to carry, hauled these canoes over their heads. It would have been one thing to carry them 100 yards, but they kept going...and going...and going. Unlike the Energizer Bunny, they became exceedingly tired extremely fast. They sweated profusely from the heavy canoes, the hot day, and walking so far. One stumbled over a root. The canoe lurched forward. It rammed the canoe ahead, causing them to ram the next one...and the next one. Picture kids, canoes, paddles, and gear strewn along the trail. Finally, they arrived at the river. They let out a "wahoo" when they dropped the canoes into the water. All of us put the gear on board, got in, pushed out into the current, and "chilled." The scenery wasn't much different than when we were walking in the woods, but it sure was a lot more enjoyable.

This story shows us what it means to be "out of Christ."

So many people struggle through life carrying the canoe over their heads, exerting incredible effort to get where they're going. The result: exhaustion, frustration, and lives strewn along the trail.

How much better to put the canoe "into (the river of) Christ," letting Him carry us. That happens when our children discover the real answer to the question "Who am I?"

Let's visualize ourselves, and especially our children, as a triangle. Each side represents a different, but important, aspect of who we are.

> With great delight God eagerly wants to show us our destiny.

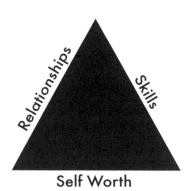

In the area of *relationships,* we may have many friends and a great family, but somewhere along the way someone is going to let us down. Facing the wounds our parents inflicted, having a friend reject us, breaking up with a boyfriend or girlfriend, dealing with divorce, all of these, and many more, can cause that side of the triangle to collapse. That is when our kids feel like klutzes—totally worthless.

In the area of *skills,* we may have many talents and abilities, but no matter how talented we are, someone—somewhere—is going to be better. Failing a test, breaking a leg playing ball,

getting fired from a job, all of these, and many other circumstances, can cause us to question *our* abilities. Then we feel
like a klutzes–totally worthless.

Both relationships and skills are important aspects of
who we are, but unless the base of the triangle is solid, our
self-worth will always be shaky because relationships and
skills will let us down. That is why it's so important to build
our self-image on the base of the triangle: *self-worth*. Self-
worth is based on who we are on the inside. For believers
that is who Christ is in us. Look at the beautiful way the
Apostle Paul describes who we are.

> Because of the sacrifice of the Messiah, his
> blood poured out on the altar of the Cross,
> we're a free people–free of penalties and
> punishments chalked up by all our
> misdeeds. And not just barely free, either.
> *Abundantly* free! He thought of everything,
> provided for everything we could possibly
> need, letting us in on the plans he took such
> delight in making. He set it all out before us
> in Christ, a long-range plan in which every-
> thing would be brought together and
> summed up in him, everything in deepest
> heaven, everything on planet earth.
>
> It's in Christ that we find out who we are
> and what we are living for. Long before we
> first heard of Christ and got our hopes up, he
> had his eye on us, had designs on us for
> glorious living, part of the overall purpose he
> is working out in everything and everyone.
> (Eph. 1:9-12, TM)

Wow! With great delight God eagerly wants to show us
and our children our destiny. He centered our destiny in
Jesus Christ. We were created to live "in Christ." If you read

Ephesians 1:1-14 and circle the phrase "in Christ," "in him," and "in the One he loves," you will circle those phrases ten times. When we live "in Christ," much more than just pursuing our future life direction is involved–we discover who He is. He is our destiny.

That changes everything! It changes the way we see ourselves, our futures, and God Himself. Instead of life being focused on me—my school, my career, my date, my marriage, and my money, it focuses on God and His destiny for us "in Christ."

Our challenge as parents is to pursue Christ passionately and let Him be our identity and self-worth. As we discover who we are and make that a part of our homes, then our children will begin to make that discovery as well.

Where Am I Going?

This is the *destination* question. Why do most students graduate from high school, and even college, with no clue about what they are going to do with their lives? They have not answered the "Where am I going?" question.

I ask high school and college students this question: "What do these things have in common? Dating. Friends. Sex. Parties. Job. College. Money." The answer: Nothing! Young people have nothing to tie all of these aspects of their lives together.

One value of knowing Jesus is that He is the focus that brings our lives together. Jesus wants us to see both God's future and present plan for us.

The flight took me (Barry) from Kansas City to Chicago, then to Winnipeg and on to Regina, Canada. From there the van drove an hour and a half down a highway through the wheat fields of western Canada. At one point the van driver

[Our children's destination: to live to reflect God's glory.]

pointed down the road and said, "Do you see that blue spot out in the distance?" I could see it easily. Not one building or tree stood between that blue roof and us. He said, "That is where we are going." It took us twenty minutes to get there! That is how far down the road we could see.

God's destination for us is like that. It is way off in the distance, but we can see it and experience it now. Nothing blocks our view. Look out in the distance. You can see it.

Three times in Ephesians 1:1-14 the Apostle Paul used the phrase *"to the praise of his glory"* (vv. 6, 12, 14). In that phrase we find our destination—both God's future and present plan for us. As we think about it, let's let God's destination grab us and create a wild enthusiasm about our family's destination—*to live to reflect His glory*.

Because we will spend eternity *reflecting His glory*, it makes sense to get in plenty of practice now. How does that work? God has given us His Holy Spirit "who is a deposit guaranteeing our inheritance..." (Eph. 1:14). A "deposit" serves as a pledge *now* that the rest of the money will be paid *later*. Because the Holy Spirit lives in us *now* as a "deposit," we can live to reflect Him *now*.

We, and others, often ask our kids, "What are you going to be when you grow up?" Depending on their interests at the time, they answer, "A fireman." "An NBA star." "A nurse." "A lawyer."

This phrase *to reflect His glory* changes our perspective. We don't need to wait until we grow up or go to heaven to reach our destination. We can reach it now, today, and every day. *To live to reflect His glory* is a lifestyle, an attitude.

How did the Apostle Paul express it in 2 Corinthians 3:18?

> But we Christians have no veil over our faces;
> we can be mirrors that brightly reflect the
> glory of the Lord. And as the Spirit of the
> Lord works within us, we become more and
> more like him. (TLB)

When we wake up and look in the mirror (bad hair and all), we need to become keenly aware that all day long we will be "mirrors" that reflect who Jesus is to other people. They will see His glory through us. They will know the attitudes, actions, and character of Jesus Christ by what they see coming out of our lives.

"Whoa!" you say. "That is heavy-duty. I can't live up to that. Nor can my children. We mess up every day. We are *not* perfect." So what else is new? The focus here is not on us. We serve only as a mirror that reflects the Holy Spirit to others. We let "the Spirit of the Lord work in us."

So what does He do in there? He gets rid of negative junk that doesn't need to be there.

> ...repetitive, loveless, cheap sex; a stinking accumulation of mental and emotional garbage; frenzied and joyless grabs for happiness; trinket gods; magic-show religion; paranoid loneliness; cutthroat competition; all-consuming-yet-never-satisfied wants; a brutal temper; an impotence to love and be loved; divided homes and divided lives; small-minded and lopsided pursuits; the vicious habit of depersonalizing everyone into a rival; uncontrolled and uncontrollable addictions; ugly parodies of community. (Gal. 5:19-21, TM)

In addition He infuses us with positive characteristics

> ...affection for others, exuberance about life, serenity....a willingness to stick with things, a sense of compassion in the heart, and a conviction that a basic holiness permeates things and people...loyal commitments, not needing to force our way in life, able to marshal and direct our energies wisely. (Gal. 5: 22-23, TM)

He produces in us and in our children the *character* of Jesus Christ. We will be able to honor Christ in our...
thoughts,
habits,
attitudes,
actions,
and relationships.

The Holy Spirit in us provides the resources for us "to become more and more like Him." The Holy Spirit takes us straight ahead to our destination: *to live to reflect His glory.*

We can't do that on our own. We don't need to jump higher, try harder, or do better. Instead, we have to call on God's resources to "just do it" in and through us. Over time He is the one who will change our thoughts, our habits, our attitudes, our actions, and our relationships so that we will be like Jesus Christ.

"In 1492 Columbus Sailed the Ocean Blue..."

Because Christopher Columbus took seriously God's destination for his life and pursued it, we have the privilege of living in North America today. Even though you have never read this in a public school text, here is the real story of how he discovered America.

After his ships had been at sea much longer than anticipated, the crew was ready to mutiny. When they confronted him wanting to turn back, Columbus prayed and then requested three more days from his crew. Immediately the wind picked up and the ships moved more swiftly than at any time before. On the evening of the third day they spotted land. He wrote in his journal later:

> It was the Lord who put it into my mind. (I could feel His hand upon me) the fact that it would be possible to sail from here to the Indies. All who heard of my project rejected

it with laughter, ridiculing me. There is no question that the inspiration was from the Holy Spirit, because He comforted me with rays of marvelous inspiration from the Holy Scriptures…I am a most unworthy sinner but I have cried out to the Lord for grace and mercy, and they have covered me completely. I have found the sweetest consolation since I made it my whole purpose to enjoy His marvelous presence. For the execution of the journey to the Indies, I did not make use of intelligence, mathematics or maps. It is simply the fulfillment of [prophecy]. [Peter Marshall Jr. and David Manuel, *The Light and the Glory,* Revell, 1977]

God's destination–*living to reflect His glory*–and His resources are the same for us and our children as they were for Christopher Columbus. Yet our destination is as uniquely significant as that of Christopher Columbus! We need to help our children see that and then pursue it with a passion!

How Am I Going to Get There?

Our family gives me (Barry) an unmercifully hard time on trips–that's because I tend to get lost. It happens a lot. Not only do I have a poor sense of direction, but I also don't use maps. I just get into the car and drive. More than once my kids have asked me, "Dad, where are we?" "Don't worry. We're cool," I respond. Upon looking at the map, we would discover that from Atlanta I had gone toward Washington when our destination was Orlando!

It's one thing to know our destiny and destination, but

[With great delight God eagerly wants to show us our destiny.]

it's another to have the specific road map with the directions and then follow those directions.

Each of us and each of our children have a unique road map that gets us to our destination and fulfills our destiny. The Apostle Paul describes how that road map works: "For we are God's workmanship, created in Christ Jesus to do good works, which God prepared in advance for us to do" (Eph. 2:10).

The word "workmanship" means "unique work of art" or "unique road map." God has prepared a unique picture in advance, a road map for us and for our children. When we are "in Christ" and desiring to "live to reflect His glory," we can pull out that map and follow it to our destination.

In our search to answer "How am I going to get there?" we have found nine "destiny deciders" that have helped us design our own unique road map. These "destiny deciders" will help you and your children create your unique road map too.

1. Personality
What is your child's personality, and how can he or she enjoy it?

Socrates said it well: "Know thyself." And we need to, but not for the reasons most people pursue knowing themselves. Our culture is saturated with self-actualization, self-improvement, self-help, and self-everything else. The dominant word in the last sentence gives us a clue as to what the problem is. Helping our children understand their personalities for selfish reasons has very little value.

Jesus put the issue of knowing ourselves on a higher plane. He said, "Love the Lord your God with all your heart...[and] love your neighbor as yourself." As we discover more about the infinite and unique personality of God, we will learn to love Him. Out of that love relationship, we will love ourselves. With a healthy love for God and ourselves, we will have the ability to love our neighbors.

The Hebrew people used the word "heart" to define personality. For example, the writer of Proverbs said, "Above all else, guard your heart, for it is the wellspring of life" (Prov. 4:23).

Out of our personality–"heart"–flows life. Therefore, we need to guard our hearts. Don't let anyone "stomp that sucker flat," as Lewis Grizzard used to say. This has particular relevance with our children's friendships and dating relationships. One of our major responsibilities is to help them build a fence around their heart so they don't give it away to the wrong people or so others don't steal it from them. We need to help them reserve it for God Himself and for that special person with whom they will spend their lives.

It's difficult to teach them to guard their hearts when they don't even know what it is. In 2400 B.C., Hippocrates, the famous philosopher/physician, identified four basic personality types. He gave names to the temperaments based on the bodily liquids that he thought was the cause: Sanguine (the influencer), Choleric (the doer), Melancholy (the thinker), and Phlegmatic (the relater). Over the years we have given our children several personality tests, which have deepened their understanding of themselves. The more they know about their personality, the more they will appreciate their uniqueness.

2. Spiritual Gifts

What is your child's spiritual gifts, and how can he or she use them?

What if you had a credit card with unlimited resources? Wow! God has issued us that kind of credit card, and we can use the card whenever we need it. Through what He gives us we have enough for ourselves and plenty left over for other people too. What a deal! Here's how it works.

GOD'S GRACE IN US
GIVES SPIRITUAL GIFTS TO US
TO ACCOMPLISH GOD'S WORK THROUGH US.

Some people are afraid of spiritual gifts. They reason: "I'm not getting into this because once you discuss spiritual gifts, then handling snakes can't be far behind." Yet without spiritual gifts we lack power to overcome the forces of darkness. With them we bring the power of Christ into any situation. Spiritual gifts are vital in discovering our destiny.

Many Christians experience lack of fulfillment because they do not know their spiritual gifts and how to use them, but when we know our spiritual gifts, we will be able to parent better and to serve Christ better. When our kids discover their gifts, they will be more motivated and spiritually alive. Many parents burn out doing God's work because they do not grasp the tremendous motivation and energy that spiritual gifts provide. Yet with these gifts in operation we have the sensitivity and ability to minister to our children, and them to us. The family will have what it takes to make a difference with our friends, in our neighborhood, on the job, and at school. That's why the Apostle Paul tells us, "Now about spiritual gifts, brothers, I do not want you to be ignorant" (1 Cor. 12:1).

Giving your children a spiritual gifts test will help them understand their spiritual gifts, and such an understanding will provide them with the opportunity to use their gifts. That will create a high degree of spiritual motivation. Moreover, doing this will supernaturally equip them to minister to their friends.

3. Abilities and Experiences

What are your child's abilities and experiences, and how can he or she maximize them?

Everything around us "suckers" us and our kids into the world's view of what we are supposed to look like, smell like, and dress like, but God does not look at our potential the way the world does.

When we look at our children's potential from a strictly human perspective, we usually fall into a ditch on either side of the road. We can have too high a view of our child's potential. We think Junior is the greatest, the most fantastic, and the best. If other parents scatter when we come around, it could be from the nausea they experience when we espouse our child's incredible talent. Conversely we can communicate to our children: "You're no good," "You will never amount to anything," or "Can't you do anything right?" Often, even when we are not saying it, that negative message gets communicated to our children. Instead of going into either ditch, I hope we can keep ourselves moving down the highway of God's perspective.

[God does not look at our potential the way the world does.]

> Do not think of yourself more highly than you ought, but rather think of yourself with sober judgment, in accordance with the measure of faith God has given you. (Rom. 12:3)

Do you ever dream about your child's future...his/her potential? Certainly! But rarely do we dream big enough. Usually we dream in light of limited abilities and confined experiences. God, however, not only wants to work through their abilities and experiences but also move beyond them.

Testing our children to determine their primary abilities and helping them discover their most significant experiences will allow them to engage in activities that will play to their strengths and minimize their weaknesses. In doing that, we help them move beyond their maximum human potential to God's supernatural potential for them.

4. Motivation
What motivates your child, and how does he or she give 100 percent?

An admirer of Teddy Roosevelt said, "Mr. Roosevelt, you are a great man." Mr. Roosevelt replied, "No, Teddy Roosevelt is a plain, ordinary man–highly motivated."

High and healthy motivation among the younger generation is in short supply these days. The prevailing philosophy of kids today is "Chill." "It doesn't matter." "No big deal." I have surveyed thousands of youth leaders about the biggest struggle they face in their youth ministries. Almost 100 percent of the time they answer "apathy." "We can motivate for fun and entertainment, but kids split when it comes to spiritual issues." What is their second biggest struggle? Parents. "They are more spiritually apathetic than the students," I hear youth leaders lament. Could there be a correlation here?

As parents, motivation must become a major focus of our attention with our children. Without it, they will go nowhere in any of the other areas we have discussed. We must take a critical look at our own motives. Then we must help our children with theirs. The Apostle Paul moves us in the right direction when he says, "Whatever you do, work at it with all your heart, as working for the Lord, not for men" (Col. 3:23).

Whether they pursue photography, business, homemaking, friendships, or any one of a thousand other interests, we need to teach them to invest every ounce of their energy into it for God's glory. To do that we must help our children move away from wrong motives, mixed motives, and weak motives to possess 100 percent, wholehearted motivation. Digging down deep to discover their motives will lead them toward total motivation. Then they can live each day with passion and enthusiasm.

5. Purpose

What is your child's life purpose, and how can he or she discover it?

An ad in *Newsweek* states, "Last year Americans traveled 350 billion miles and never found what they were looking for."

Without purpose we are like the turnpike close to my (Barry's) childhood home in West Virginia. It's the turnpike that "starts nowhere and ends nowhere." Without purpose we're traveling but going nowhere.

As a parent and youth leader I agree with Albert Camus, the philosopher: "Here is what frightens me. To see the sense of this life dissipated; to see our reason for existence disappear. That is what is intolerable. Man cannot live without meaning."

In my speaking to thousands of students each year, I estimate that 90 percent of the Christian young people I talk to have no sense of purpose. Think about it. Where can they discover their purpose? No secular high school or college curriculum teaches values, much less helps young people with their purpose. Rarely do churches or Christian schools address the subject specifically. So how do our children discover it? They don't unless they either "happen on it" or learn it from us as parents. Out of that vacuum we have the great privilege of helping our kids discover their purpose.

Our children's purpose is their target. If they miss it, they miss the entire reason for their existence. For that reason we need to work with them to develop their one-sentence life purpose.

6. Values

What are your child's values, and how can he or she define them?

We live in a post-Christian era, which has created a values vacuum. Violence, drugs, alcohol, and teenage sex scream at us daily in the entertainment and news media. Yet no one seems to know how to stop us from sliding down the slippery slope. As parents we must put our finger into the dike and do our part to stem the tide of the values vacuum. We can do that with our children, in our churches, and through our own sphere of influence.

What is a "value"? The Apostle Paul describes a value as what we "set our hearts on" and what we "set our minds on"

(Col. 3:2). What we live for and think about is what we value. When we value something, we honor it, we love it, and we hold it in high esteem. A value is a quality, object, or person that we look at and say, "That is important."

For followers of Christ, Jesus is our "core value." He is at the center of our value system because our lives are "now hidden with Christ in God" (Col. 3:3). We can help our children discover their six core values. When they have these in writing and begin to live by them, then what they believe (value) will begin to match up with how they behave. When that happens, they will be a long way down the road in charting their own unique course.

7. Goals
What are your child's goals, and how can he or she reach them?

One of the most intense complaints I hear from youth leaders is that their kids are too busy. One parent of three teenagers told me last week, "By the time we get to the weekend, my kids are so exhausted that they sleep half the day and then sit around staring into space. They are pooped from the pace." Someone called that "the barrenness of busyness." The results are not only that our families are exhausted but also that we do many good things that keep us from doing God's best things. When we teach our children to set goals that connect to their purpose and values, they will know why they are doing the things they do.

Mike Philips challenges us to define our goals clearly:

> There's a lot of verbal "fog" floating around in Christian circles because of fuzzy ill-defined purposes and goals. We talk about giving God glory, taking the gospel into the world, and living God-honoring lives. But as long as such statements remain undefined, they are useless. [Mike Philips, *Getting More Done in Less Time*, Bethany House, 1982, p. 55]

Every goal we set, large or small, should enhance our values and move us toward our life purpose. For years I knew this must be true, but I didn't know how to make that connection. Now I know. And you can too. We simply work with our children to set yearly goals. Then each month we review those yearly goals and set monthly goals to accomplish them. Then each morning in their quiet time they can review their monthly goals and set their goals for that day. That way each day they are accomplishing God's long-term and short-term plans for their lives.

8. Time
What time does your child have, and how does he or she use it?

> Time, unlike money, cannot be saved, only spent. No saving for a rainy day, we must spend every second *now*. Yesterday is a cancelled check. Tomorrow is a promissory note. Today must be spent wisely. [Edward R. Dayton and Ted W. Engstrom, *Strategy for Living*, Regal Books, 1976]

The average American, who lives seventy years, spends his time similar to this:

23 years sleeping
19 years working
9 years playing
6 years traveling
6 years eating
4 years sick
2 years dressing
1 year in church

We spend 69/70th of life on temporal things and only 1/70th pursuing our eternal destiny.

We say, "My, how time flies." And it does. Soon our children will be gone. That is why this discussion is extremely significant. We need to seriously consider whether or not our families are spending their time wisely. Our parental responsibility is not to make our children more or less busy but to help them find meaningful balance. If we help them keep a record of the way they spend their time using a daily time log, they will discover how and where they waste their time. Then we can work with them on their ideal schedule, which will include the goals they have set. This way we can help them use their time in a way that reflects their goals and values and moves them toward their life purpose.

9. Decisions
What decisions does your child need to make, and how will he or she make them?

Most children think their decisions have *no consequences*. Yet as parents we know better. The earlier they learn to make decisions the better, because this adage is true:

We make our decisions. Then our decisions make us.

That begins to manifest itself in the teenage years. Between the ages of sixteen and twenty-two our kids will make the decisions that will cause them to experience the most dramatic and permanent changes in their lives. Dr. James Dobson says,

> Most of the decisions that will shape the next fifty years will be made in this era, including the choice of occupation, perhaps the decision to marry, and the establishment of values and principles by which life will be governed. What makes this period even more significant is the impact of early mistakes and errors in judgment. They can

undermine all that is to follow. [James Dobson, *Life on the Edge*, Word, 1995, p. 3]

The very thought of this frightens us as parents. We would give anything to make our children's decisions for them. (And many parents of teenagers are still trying!) But we know that is not right, healthy, or even possible. Yet we can guide them and teach them to know how to make their own decisions, and to do so wisely.

One of several tools I use to do this is the **STEPS** approach.

See the goal clearly.
Take in the facts.
Evaluate the alternatives.
Project strengths and weaknesses.
Select the best alternative.

Making decisions this way will give our children the sense that every day they are making decisions that move them toward their goals, values, purpose, and then ultimately to God's destiny for their lives.

Integrity
The end result of all of this is integrity. Integrity comes from the math word *integer*, a whole–all of the fractions add up to a whole number. When our children deal with each of these issues, then they will be integrated. All of the pieces of their lives will add up to the whole. They will have integrity. Our job as parents is to take all of these different parts and to shape our children into the whole person they were created to be. Then they will live out their unique destiny.

Taking Action

Write the approach you want to take to communicate the "destiny deciders" to your child. Consider where, when, and how you will do that.

Penetrating Questions

1. Do you personally have clear-cut answers to the questions: Who am I? Where am I going? How am I going to get there?

2. As a parent do you understand and live out your destiny "in Christ"?

3. In parenting your children, what are you doing that is moving you and your family toward the destination of "living to reflect His glory"?

4. Of the nine "destiny deciders," which ones do you have a clear direction on for yourself? For your children?

5. What do you need to do to prepare to lead your children through the nine "destiny deciders"?

Fresh Ideas

•   Think about this as a long-term rather than a short-term project.

•   Consider weekly conversations with your child about these topics, using it as an opportunity for long-term discipleship with your child. (*Life Happens: Help Your Teenager Get Ready* has prepared these discussions for you.)

•   Decide on a fun activity each week that will go along with your serious discussions.

- Meet with a group of parents regularly to discuss how you can support one another and your children in accomplishing this. (*Life Happens: Help Your Teenager Get Ready* has prepared these discussions for your group.)

- Order the material you need now.

Further Reading
Dobson, James. *Life on the Edge*. Dallas: Word, 1995.

St. Clair, Barry. *Life Happens: Get Ready*. Nashville: Broadman & Holman, 1997. (Describes the "destiny deciders" in much greater depth and provides a practical tool with each one to help discover it.)

St. Clair, Barry. *Life Happens: Help Your Teenager Get Ready*, Nashville: Broadman & Holman, 1997. (The parent's guide.)

Look for God in the Ups and Downs

How can our children build confidence in God through life's exciting and disappointing experiences?

SCOTT HAD A SORE THROAT AND FEVER, but that wasn't enough to keep him from playing in his high school basketball tournament that weekend. On Sunday night his fever shot up. Then early in the morning we heard him crying out for us. Hurrying downstairs, we found him violently ill. As we rushed to get him to the hospital, he collapsed on the way by the door. An already bad day only got worse. The doctors put him on a respirator. They diagnosed him with a staph infection, which resulted in double pneumonia. Scott asked me pointedly, "Dad, can I die?"

That night I asked some men from our church to come to the hospital to pray for Scott. We gathered around his bed. My athletic son, who only two days before played basketball, lay comatose in the bed with needles stuck in his body, each one leading to a bank of machines behind his bed. It was eerie. Five men dressed in yellow hospital gowns and masks gathered around my son and prayed, following the instructions of James 5:14-16. The Lord impressed on us specifically what to pray:

- That the Lord would dramatically change Scott's physical condition overnight so the hospital personnel could see God's hand at work.
- That God would reveal Himself to Scott in his subconscious mind.

I slept fitfully that night. The next morning the nurse greeted me with these words: "The difference in Scott's lungs between last night and this morning is like night and day. It's a miracle!"

When I went into his room, Scott wrote on a tablet (he couldn't talk because of the tube):

> The other day the news reports said that the number of *deaths* from the flu and pneumonia had reached the point of epidemic proportions. When I found out about double pneumonia, it threw me for a loop. Lately my Christian walk had not been growing but was at a standstill. Last night the Lord changed my view of Him, the world, and myself. He put His vibrant Spirit wholeheartedly back into me. I woke up today praising the Lord just to be alive. I am exalting Him. Every

time the nurses woke me up to do testing,
they said I had a great big smile on my face.
I woke up singing, "This is the day the Lord
has made…"

Then Scott wrote in large letters: "PRAISE THE LORD!"

Yet it wasn't over. Although God had performed a miracle to save his life that night, Scott spent eighteen days in the hospital. His weight dropped from 155 pounds to 127 pounds. Ten days later, after he spent his sixteenth birthday in the hospital, I walked into his room, and he broke down and cried:

> Dad, bear with me. I just need to pour my
> heart out to the Lord. Lord, I'm so frustrated.
> I'm sick of everybody telling me how sick I
> am. I want to get up and get out of here now.
> But, Lord, You are the Author and Finisher of
> my faith. You are in charge of my life. You
> can do anything you want. You can make me
> well in five minutes or five years. I want you
> to know that I trust you whatever.

We held each other and cried. Then through the tears he began to sing:

> My God is an awesome God.
> He reigns from heaven above,
> with wisdom, power, and love.
> My God is an awesome God.

That was the most harrowing experience of our parenting years. Even now when we talk about it, tears flow. Yet from that Scott discovered his destiny. Since then he has pursued God wholeheartedly. Out of it has come the strong calling to medicine–a pediatrician, no less!

When the Bottom Drops Out...

Have you ever carried a bag of groceries that somehow
became wet on the bottom? Suddenly, the bottom drops out.
The boxes, cans, and bottles scatter across the parking lot.
Frustrated, we want to kick them–hard. And yell. And get
angry. But what good does that do?

As parents we want everything to work out perfectly for
our children. We desire to spare them hurt and heartache.
But that's impossible. Childhood and adolescence has many
ups and downs. The bottom *will* drop out. Each of our children has experienced some trauma that seemed terrible at
the time, but God has used it for good.

> There is nothing
> –no circumstance, no trouble, no testing–
> that can ever touch me until,
> first of all it has gone past God and past Christ,
> right through to me.
>
> If it has come that far,
> it has come with great purpose
> which I may not understand at the moment.
> But as I refuse to become panicky,
> as I lift up my eyes to Him
> and accept it as coming from the throne of God
> for some great purpose of blessing to my own heart,
> no sorrow will ever disturb me,
> no trial will ever disarm me,
> no circumstances will cause me to fret,
> for I shall rest in the joy of Who my Lord is.
>
> —Alan Redpath

So how do we help our children look for God in the
pain? How do we prepare them to see that through the difficulty God is working out His perfect plan for their lives?

Before going to Psalm 34 for some answers, let's look at

the backdrop of the psalm so we can know the questions. At the same time David wrote the psalm, his life was like a yo-yo. In 1 Samuel 18–22, we find a young man in the midst of incredible intrigue. Anger, jealousy, fear, manipulation, love and sex, in-laws, and war. This is better than a plot line on the hottest soap opera.

This sad saga began with Saul's promotion of David through the ranks of his army. David, equal to the task, became remarkably successful and well liked. The trouble started after one campaign when the crowds chanted, "Saul has slain his thousands, and David his tens of thousands" (1 Sam. 18:7). It all began to unravel when Saul became exceedingly jealous. The open door of jealousy allowed an evil spirit to come upon him. That spirit caused Saul to attack David by throwing his spear at him while David played his harp for Saul. Because Saul feared David's success, he set out to destroy him. As a result David lost everything he had gained–except God and his character.

David lost his position (1 Sam. 19:8-17). Saul had this thing about throwing spears. While David played the harp, Saul threw it again. David escaped to his house, but Saul came to kill him. David did the "dummy in the bed" trick, which fooled Saul into thinking David was asleep, but David was long gone. So was his position of favor with Saul.

Amazingly, some people will not like our children. Like David, people will turn against them, throw "spears" at them, and will cause them to lose out. It might be grades because a teacher doesn't like them. It could be a coach who keeps them on the bench when they deserve to play. Maybe an older student turns against them, and they lose popularity or get a black eye. Possibly a boss fires them. Something like this *will* happen and probably several times. We need to prepare our children to deal with such adversity.

David was disappointed by his spiritual leader (1 Sam. 19:18). Frustrated and disappointed, David sought out his mentor, Samuel. We don't know the total conversation, but we do know that David "told him all that Saul had done to him." Attempted murder, deception, bribery, and manipulation had left David disillusioned with his spiritual leader, his king.

People of influence in our children's lives will disappoint them. It might be a Sunday School teacher who cuts them down. Possibly a youth leader they trust leaves. Maybe the church splits. Every one of those examples has happened to our family. Inevitably they will happen in yours as well. Our children need to know how to respond correctly during those kinds of disappointments.

David was separated from his best friend (1 Sam. 20:1-42). David and Jonathan were closer than blood brothers. Saul's actions, however, drove a wedge between them. After another spear-tossing incident, Jonathan met David in a field to tell him that Saul, his father, had placed a bounty on David's head. Feel the pathos of this separation as you read:

> Then they kissed each other and wept together–but David wept the most. Jonathan said to David, "Go in peace, for we have sworn friendship with each other in the name of the Lord." (1 Sam. 20:41-42)

Deep hurt will come to our children in relationships. Count on it. A close friend could move away. Maybe a "best friend" rejects them. Possibly a boyfriend or girlfriend breaks their hearts. Perhaps we hurt them by getting a divorce–often wounding our children so deeply that it takes them a lifetime to get over it. (That is one reason God is against divorce.) Whatever the cause, our children need to know how to handle deep hurt.

When these kinds of things happen, our children naturally want to place blame on someone or something. Often they get mad at God and blame Him. Sometimes they blame themselves. Many times they run from the problem and try to hide. David responded like that. Mad at God, he lost his confidence and self-respect. He started running and kept on running (1 Sam. 21).

By the time we catch up with him again, the bottom has dropped out completely. His life is at its lowest point. Not only is he disappointed, hurt, afraid, and lonely, but he is also living like an animal in the back of a cave (1 Sam. 22:1).

Our parenting experience shows that at one time or another, God drives every person to the point. Mickey Evans began Dunklin Memorial Camp in rural south Florida to reach drug addicts and alcoholics for Christ. One of the down-and-outers that Mickey ministered to prompted our friend, Ken Helser, to write this song:

"Broke, But Not Quite Broken"
Out on the range they call me cowboy,
I ride high in the saddle like a man.
I could drink, I could fight, I could stay out all night,
'Til trouble finally lent a helping hand.
I woke up all hung over in a jailhouse.
I cried, Lord, this is more than I can stand.
My last dime got through to Dunklin,
They had a bed that I could bunk in.
I said, "Mickey, I'm in trouble.
Can you give the boy a hand?"

He said, "You're broke, but not quite broken.
How you gonna hear the Lord when He has spoken?
Cause being broke, but not quite broken...
You're gonna run away when the door flies open."

Just a proud, crazy, old cowboy.
A ladies' man, riding high in style.
I could dance 'em and romance 'em,
And then hang 'em out to dry...
Pretend I even loved some for a while.

'Til I tied the knot with one that had my baby,
Thought maybe this would tame the cowboy down.
'Til my mind flipped back to Dunklin,
And the only thing that sunk in,
Was the last thing Mickey told me,
When He loved me with his smile...

He said, "You're broke, but not quite broken,
How you gonna hear the Lord when He has spoken?
Cause being broke, but not quite broken...
You're gonna run away when the door flies open."

Now one day, this proud, crazy, cowboy
Lost it all to women, drugs, and gin.
And no matter where I turned, I was always gettin'
    burned,
'Til I remembered something Mickey called...
"LOST-IN-SIN!"
So I picked up my Bible, started reading,
Saw something I had never seen before.
Scales fell from my eyes.
I began to realize.
Gotta get back to Dunklin, cause I really need you Lord.

Now I'm broke, and I'm finally broken.
I cry every time my Lord has spoken.
Lord, take my heart, and break it wide open.
Cause more than being broke...I wanna be broken.

When our children are "in the pits" of brokenness, what
can we bring to the darkness of the cave to encourage them
to look up and see the sunshine of God? That's where Psalm
34 comes in. David wrote this psalm in the cave at the lowest
point of his life. In "the pits" he decided to go on a "God
Hunt"–looking for God in every situation. As a result, he

found God *and* the solutions to his difficulties and disappointments.

Focus on God through Praise
When we have problems, praise God. That sounds naïve, oversimplified, and even ridiculous, but from parenting experience it is not "pie in the sky" advice. Each of our children has experienced some trauma that seemed terrible at the time, but God has used it for good. Katie tore her ACL and broke up with her boyfriend in the same year. Jonathan and Katie were involved in a death-defying wreck. Shifting our focus took tremendous concentration. So we followed David's example.

David found himself in the cave's darkness with his life "caving in" around him. Certainly he had a right to a pity party or at least an anxiety appetizer. With overwhelming problems, his natural response was similar to ours.

We GAZE at the problem and GLANCE at God.

But by the time he wrote Psalm 34, David had decided to take God's route out of the cave. And we can too when…

We GAZE at God and GLANCE at the problem.

David consciously took his eyes off of his circumstances and instead lifted his face to the Heavenly Father in praise.

> I will extol the Lord at all times;
> his praise will always be on my lips.
> My soul will boast in the Lord;
> let the afflicted hear and rejoice.
> Glorify the Lord with me;
> let us exalt his name together. (Ps. 34:1-3)

We struggle with the praise approach for two reasons.

1. *We focus so much on circumstances that we lose perspective.* Recently our Katie got married. On the wedding morning the "table and chair" company had promised to arrive at 9:30 A.M. At 10:15 they still had not come. I (Barry) called to "move the process along," but I received no help, and we were running out of time. About then they showed up and I lost it.

[

We need to

GAZE at God

and GLANCE at

the problem.

Certainly we can all relate. So do our kids. They can get "in a wad" as easily as we do. In those situations God is shut out. Whether our difficulty is big or small, our best bet is to stop, force our faces toward heaven, and say, "Jesus, You are Lord in this situation. Right now, I praise You."

2. *We don't feel comfortable praising the Lord.* People come from different religious backgrounds and expressions of worship. Whatever our background God desires from us unrestrained worship. Praise is an action that expresses worship. Worship ascribes *worth* to something. It comes from inside of us. Praise gives outward expression to our inward worship. Most of the time we think of praise as something we do at church when we sing. That's partially true. I love to teach teenagers to sing "Clap Your Hands." Each time we add a new expression of praise from a verse in a psalm, then we put that action into the song.

- Psalm 145:10-11. *Speak.*
- Psalm 146:1-2. *Sing.*
- Psalm 47:1. *Clap.*
- Psalm 47:1. *Shout.*
- Psalm 123:1. *Lift our eyes.*
- Psalm 134:1-2. *Lift our hands.*
- Psalm 149:3. *Dance.*

Imagine thousands of teenagers doing all of those things

at once. It's wild! But then a hush of appreciation comes over the crowd when I give them permission to freely express praise anytime anywhere! To help our families become comfortable expressing praise, we recommend giving children mega-opportunities to express praise in family settings and then encouraging them to express it anytime anywhere.

Nevertheless, singing or doing any other acts of worship in church is only a small part of it. Praise is a something we do in every action and attitude every day. How I talk to the person across the counter at the store is an act of praise (or nonpraise depending how I treat that person). The list of ways we can praise the Lord is as long as the actions we take from the time we wake up until we go to bed. Modeling that kind of praise for our children is one of the greatest gifts we can give to them.

Once past these two barriers we can begin to create a powerful spiritual reservoir of praise for those difficult times when our children feel as though God does not exist or that He has let them down. In addition, we want to create that reservoir for the good times, because often that is when they forget God and think they have everything under control. Building a reservoir of worship at home will help them keep their focus on God in good and bad times.

How do we create that "worship reservoir" in our children? We help them grasp the *greatness of God*. One of three primary names of God used in the Old Testament is *Elohim*. That name expresses God's greatness. We get an idea of how vast that greatness is from verses like Psalm 95:3-5 and Psalm 145:3-4.

> For the Lord is the great God,
> the great King above all gods.
> In his hand are the depths of the earth,
> and the mountain peaks belong to him.
> The sea is his, for he made it,
> and his hands formed the dry land.

> Great is the Lord and most worthy of praise;

> his greatness no one can fathom.
> One generation will commend your works to
> another;
> they will tell of your mighty acts.

Notice the significant role of parents in communicating the greatness of God. Parents are to "show and tell" the mighty acts of God to their children. When we talk to them about the greatness of God, we can tell them that the name *Elohim* is used 2,700 times in the Old Testament, 32 times in Genesis 1 alone in connection with creation. He is the great Creator God. In contrast to us:

> We create something out of something.
> God creates something out of nothing.

We can show them from nature that when He creates, He does it magnificently.

On a beach in Mexico I (Barry) stretched my legs preparing to go for a run. I did not want to be there. My dad was very sick with cancer, and I had brought him there for treatment. I felt extremely discouraged. As I stretched, I faced a rock wall. As I looked up, it towered above me at least one hundred feet. I said out loud, "That's huge!" Then I looked around. On the left stood a mountain with clouds surrounding it, but the peak protruded out the top of the clouds. Turning around and looking behind me, I saw the Pacific Ocean with the waves crashing and the sun setting. Overwhelmed with God's bigness and my smallness, I yelled out, "God, You are great!"

All kids are impressed with *bigness*. They can get some idea of God's bigness when they realize that if they could travel thirty-seven round trips of the United States per second, they would pass the moon in 1.5 seconds. They would pass the sun in eight seconds. In one day they would pass out of the solar system. It would take 10,000 years to leave our galaxy and two million years to get to Andromeda, one of a half a dozen galaxies close to ours. By any defini- tion—God's universe is big!

When our children go on a "God Hunt," they'll discover how creative, great, and big God is. Then they can respond to Him as *Elohim*—the mighty, powerful, tran- scendent God. Their response: WORSHIP.

> Come, let us bow down in worship,
> let us kneel before the Lord our Maker;
> for he is our God [Elohim]
> and we are the people of his pasture,
> the flock under his care. (Ps. 95:6-7)

> When our children worship the greatness of God, they can handle any difficulty.

No more will this world's idols rule our kids' lives when they hunt for, find, and kneel in worship to *Elohim*!

Seek the Lord in Prayer

Often prayer becomes trivialized and boring for our children. Driving down the freeway in Oregon today, I (Barry) passed a sign that said, "Boring—11 miles." Growing up in church, I knew it wasn't that far! I hated being bored so much as a kid that when I began to work with students I decided I would never bore kids with the Gospel. Because prayer was the most boring, I turned to God only when I was desperate—like when a game was on the line and I was shooting a free throw.

But prayer doesn't have to bore kids. A few days ago I led 700 high school students in a prayer meeting that lasted for two-and-a-half hours. It seemed as if it had lasted only two- and-a-half minutes! Thirty minutes after we adjourned, half the people were still praying. Our challenge: to make communicating with God so real and exciting that prayer captivates our children. When we do that, they can come up against any circumstance, no matter how difficult, and know that God answers prayer.

Certainly David experienced that in the cave. In the midst of this "my life is falling apart" phase of his life, David turned to God and had an honest talk, telling Him his exact needs. God heard and answered.

> I sought the Lord, and he answered me; he delivered me from all my fears. Those who look to him are radiant; their faces are never covered with shame. This poor man called, and the Lord heard him; he saved him out of all his troubles. (Ps. 34:4-6)

Prayer is indeed a "God Hunt." The question is: How can we help our children find Him?

1. *See prayer as our communication channel with God.* Jesus had constant communication with His Father. That communication directed His every action every day.

> Jesus gave them this answer: "I tell you the truth, the Son can do nothing by himself; he can do only what he sees his Father doing, because whatever the Father does the Son also does. For the Father loves the Son and shows him all he does." (John 5:19-20)

Praying with our children, we need to enter into dynamic communication with the Father as Jesus did. As we pray about daily activities and attitudes, our children will eventually learn to "pray continually" (1 Thes. 5:17). That way they know what the Father wants them to do at any given moment. That makes prayer exceptionally dynamic, as the following story illustrates.

We met Richard and T.C. Bailey while equipping youth leaders. All of us talked about our children. We told him that our Katie wanted to attend Furman University. The Lord kept that in Richard's mind, and he told Karen, a girl in his youth group, who also planned to attend Furman, about Katie. The Lord kept Katie's name tucked away in Karen's mind. After Karen arrived at Furman on the first day, she wanted to find Katie.

Meanwhile, Katie had prayed that the first day she would meet some Christians who would become close friends. Karen and some friends from Montgomery, Alabama, headed for the campus picnic. Our family was walking to the campus picnic as well. Someone mentioned our name out loud. Karen and her friends were walking by and heard "St. Clair." Karen squealed in freshman girl fashion, "Are you Katie St. Clair?" They met and became fast friends. The fascinating twist to the story is that among Karen's friends that day was a freshman football player named Bart. Katie and Bart Garrett also became friends—and got married when they graduated!

Simple sensitivity to hear God changed lives for generations. That's dynamic prayer!

2. *Engage in prayer that pushes back the kingdom of darkness and advances the Kingdom of Light.* Satan has taken ground that doesn't belong to him. We do not have the power to do anything about that—that is, outside of the Holy Spirit empowering us. He who is in us is greater than he who is in the world (1 John 4:4). We can push back the kingdom of darkness and bring in the kingdom of light through our prayers. When the Apostle Paul tells us to put on the armor of God "so that you can take your stand against the devil's schemes" (Eph. 6:11), he lists prayer as the last piece of armor. "And pray in the Spirit on all occasions with all kinds of prayers and requests. With that in mind, be alert and

always keep on praying for all the saints" (v. 18).

If ever this understanding of prayer was relevant for parents, it is now! Never in history has a generation been bombarded with temptations like our children's generation. The entertainment media, schools, kids next door, adults who influence their lives–they all are trying to lure them into sex, alcohol, drugs, rebellion, suicide, and other destructive behavior. How else can we describe that except as an onslaught of Satan!

Prayer serves as the weapon with which we fight. We must teach our children to use this weapon early. Then they will be prepared when they get into junior high and high school. That preparation is as simple as praying with our children every morning and night over every issue that comes up that is a struggle or temptation. Later when the pressure is greater, they will have sharpened the tool that can handle struggles and temptations correctly.

One night in high school Scott came into our bedroom late after spending the evening with friends. He told us he felt bad because he had seen a movie he should not have seen. "What movie?" we asked. "*The Exorcist*," he answered. He explained how he felt caught in the situation and made a bad decision. We did not overreact (our natural response). Instead, all three of us dropped to our knees and prayed for protection from Satan against Scott. An explosive situation turned into a "God Hunt."

How do we capture our kids with this kind of exciting prayer–the kind that brings victory? We show them through experience that God really does answer prayer. We help them trust in the One Who Is Present To Meet Every Need. *Jehovah* is another of the three primary names of God in the Old Testament, and He is called *Jehovah* 6,800 times.

When *Jehovah* met Moses at the burning bush, His presence was so awesome that Moses "was afraid to look at God" (Ex. 3:6). But God told Moses, "I have heard them crying out...I am concerned about their suffering. So I have *come down to rescue them*" (vv. 7-8, italics added). Then Moses asked God what to tell the Israelites when they ask, "What is his name?" (v. 13). God told Moses to tell them, "I am who I am" (v. 14). That name, *Jehovah,* expresses His desire to meet every need that we have through His presence.

Children relate to what is concrete rather than abstract. They want to see, touch, and feel. They want God to be with them. That's what makes Jehovah so attractive to children.

The Father *is* present.

The Son *is* a person.

The Spirit *is* power.

Kids can relate to that reality. Taking this one step further, *Jehovah* gave Himself names that address every need that we have. We can tell our children:

- If we need *resources*, then *Jehovah-Jireh* is our PROVIDER (Gen. 22:14; John 1:29; Phil. 4:19).
- If we need *healing*, then *Jehovah-Rophe* is our HEALTH (Ex. 15:26).
- If we struggle with *lust*, then *Jehovah-Nissi* is our VICTORY (Ex. 17:15; John 12:32).
- If we are *anxious*, then *Jehovah Shalom* is our PEACE (Jud. 6:23-24; Phil. 4:6-7).
- If we experience *injustice*, then *Jehovah-Tsidkenu* is our RIGHTEOUSNESS (Jer. 23:5-6; 2 Cor. 5:21).
- If we feel *lonely*, then *Jehovah-Shamah* is PRESENT (Ezek. 48:35; 1 Cor. 3:16).
- If we feel *guilty*, then *Jehovah-M'Keddesh* is our SANCTI-FIER (Lev. 20:7-8; 1 Peter 1:15-16).
- If we face *decisions*, then *Jehovah-Rohi* is our GUIDE (Ps. 23:1; John 10:27).
- If we face *danger*, then *Jehovah-Sabaot* is our PROTEC-TOR (1 Sam. 1:3; 2 Thes. 3:3).

In the seven years my dad had cancer, his adult children cried out to God like little kids. We prayed simple, childlike prayers on his behalf. When we decided to take him to Mexico for treatment, we had no tickets, no place to stay, a different language and culture to deal with, and a doctor we did not know. We prayed that Jehovah-Jireh would provide. And provide He did! We received three free airline tickets. My friend, Josh McDowell, offered a house–not just any house, but a cozy cottage on the cliffs overlooking the Pacific Ocean only ten minutes from the doctor's office! And the doctor was so kind and helpful that he came to us. In fact, the first time this doctor came, he almost scared my mother out of her skin when he knocked on the glass door, because she wasn't used to doctors making house calls.

Jehovah–The One Who Is Present To Meet Every Need did just that. And it added at least ten months to my dad's life. Every one of these nine "need meeting" names became reality because *Jehovah*, as He had with Moses, heard us cry out, let us know He was concerned about us, and came down to rescue us.

Teaching our children to go on a "God Hunt" for the One Whose Presence Meets All Of Our Needs will lead them to TRUST Him. They will know *Jehovah's* many-faceted personality from practical experience.

[**When our children experience the presence of God, they can handle any problem.**]

Choose to Submit to God's Control

In today's culture nobody wants to submit to anybody. That makes teaching our children to experience God's power through submission doubly difficult.

Two monsters stare down at parents, but we must bring those monsters to their knees. Then submission to Jesus as Lord can become a reality in our children's lives. These monsters are:

• Accepting authority.

It's pretty common to hear comments like the following coming from kids:

—"It's not fair."
—"You can't make me."
—"No, I will not."
—"I've got a right."
—"I'm not your slave."

• Sorting out selfishness.

I like to pull out a $20 bill and ask a group of students what they would do if I gave it to them. Inevitably the answer revolves around something like buying pizza or getting new clothes. Rarely does anyone mention giving it to a homeless person, to the church, or even to a friend. Selfishness is ingrained in us. Indeed, children choose selfishly. To the degree that our children are rebellious and selfish, they cannot experience God.

Enter *Adonai*–the King who sits on His throne, ruling and reigning! He wants to do in our children's lives what He did with David in the cave. Humbled through difficult experiences, David accepted God's control over them. *Adonai*, the third primary name for God in the Old Testament, did such a deep work in David's life through these difficult circumstances that David came to know Him much more intimately. That's why he could exclaim with enthusiasm:

Taste and see that the Lord is good;
blessed is the man who takes refuge in him.
Fear the Lord, you his saints,
for those who fear him lack nothing.
(Ps. 34:8-9)

Emptying himself of himself led David to "taste" the awesomeness of God with intimate reverence. That impacted him so deeply that he realized that with *Adonai*, he "lacked nothing."

One teenager's T-shirt summarized *Adonai* well:

GOD RULZ!

If our children get into a "cave" as David did, we can be encouraged. God will use it to humble them until they accept authority, and to break them of selfishness. Everything in us wants to bail them out of tough situations. Giving in to that temptation short-circuits the humbling and breaking that will bring them to their knees and cause them to call God *Adonai*–the King who sits on His throne–ruling and reigning in their lives. God will use the difficult experiences in our children's lives to help them get to know *Adonai*.

[**When our children submit to the control of God, they can handle any disappointment.**]

When Katie was in high school, I saw her cry twice–when she tore her ACL ligament and when her boyfriend broke up with her. We watched God take her through a terribly painful, breaking process that lasted two years. She struggled. She hurt. But she tasted the Lord and was blessed by Him, and He created an intimate reverence in her for *Adonai*. God did such a deep work that it changed her life forever.

Katie's journal at Furman University, fall 1995:

Lord, I do not understand why you have chosen to strip away all the different parts of my life. I have felt so hurt and so alone. But you have quieted my heart to hear your voice–describing your amazing love and grace. I have seen your character in your Word and through prayer. May I never forget what you have taught me. I want to be refined and to know that you are in control. I surrender all!

Taking Action

Applying what we have discovered, go on a "God Hunt." Explain it to your children at their age level. Then around meals, at bedtime, driving, or in any conversation, ask variations of the question: "Where do you see God in this situation?" Then praise Him, pray to Him, and submit to Him! Begin the habit of journaling your "God Hunt" insights. Later go back and review them together as a family.

Penetrating Questions

1. In what way has "the bottom dropped out" for each of your children?

2. Do you believe the Alan Redpath quote on page 180?

3. On a scale of 1 to 10, how would you assess your family's expression of unrestrained worship?

4. What traditions, background, or experiences are keeping you from expressing unrestrained worship?

5. Practically, what can your family do to experience a greater degree of unrestrained worship?

6. In what ways have you seen "The God Who Is Present To Meet Your Needs" answer those needs as you have prayed?

7. From what you learned in this chapter, how can you lead your family in making prayer a more exciting experience?

8. What one area does each person in your family struggle with in letting God take control? What is your game plan to let Him rule and reign in that?

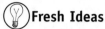**Fresh Ideas**

- You and your spouse note where the bottom has dropped out for each of your children. Design a "game plan" to help your children see God in it.

- Have a family meeting to talk about the "God Hunt." Have your children discover the background of Psalm 34 from 1 Samuel 18–22. Memorize one verse of Psalm 34 together each week. Talk about where they see God in the difficulties of their lives.

- Buy several CDs of praise music. Play them at home. If you have teenagers, buy the ones they want. Play the praise music in the car, giving each person equal time for his or her favorites. Use the words to the praise songs for discussion.

- Set the example of unrestrained worship. Because your children will feel awkward at first, let them enter into this at their own pace.

- To make prayer exciting for your children, use a variety of prayer methods. *An Awesome Way to Prayer* material will help tremendously (see this chapter's "Further Reading").

- Pray God's protection from Satan over your children every day. Put the spiritual armor on them (Eph. 6:10-18). Take Communion as a family, praying Revelation 12:11 for them. Ask God's angels to go with them, praying Psalm 34:7 for them.

- Identify one area where your children insist on being in control. Pray specifically for God to break them and give them the desire to submit to His control.

- Go on a "God Hunt" yourself by having a quiet time every day and then looking for God in every situation during the day. Report to your family what you discover.

Further Reading

Arthur, Kay. *Lord, I Want to Know You*. Portland, Ore.: Multnomah Press, 1996.

Bounds, E. M. *Power Through Prayer*. Chicago: Moody Press, 1979.

St. Clair, Barry. *An Awesome Way to Pray*. Nashville: Lifeway Press, 1998. Includes a leader's guide and student journal. The leader's guide will give you a unique approach and mega-ideas on how to creatively involve your children in prayer.

St. Clair, Barry. *Spending Time Alone with God*. Atlanta: Reach Out Youth Solutions, 1991.

Measure Success by God's Vision

**How can we help our children live the
Kingdom Dream instead of the American Dream?**

AFTER KATIE TURNED THIRTEEN, I took her to
Minneapolis. I spoke at "Something's Happening USA," a
prayer conference for high school students. The first night
we sat in the back corner of the hotel ballroom. A few seats
remained. After a few minutes Bill and Vonette Bright of
Campus Crusade for Christ sat down with us.

The format of the evening consisted of many opportunities for small-group praying. Katie found herself in a group of

three with the Brights. The rest of the week when I was not speaking, we sat in the back corner. When the Brights were there, they sat in the same corner. Numerous times over the week Katie prayed and talked with the Brights. They gave her personal attention, encouragement, and prayer. At thirteen she had no idea of the spiritual depth and world impact of these great leaders. Yet as her dad, I watched with amazement and gratefulness at the precious prayers they prayed for her. Only the Lord knows the "rubbing off" effect they had on her.

What Katie did not know was that when Bill and Vonette were new believers, they drew up a list outlining what they wanted in life. Those desires were mainly directed toward worldly gain and comfort. They then decided to reassess their list in light of their new faith, writing down things like "living holy lives," being "effective witnesses for Christ," and "helping fulfill the Great Commission in this generation." Then they consecrated these priorities in the form of a "written contract" with the Lord. In this document they renounced materialistic desires, surrendered their lives, and took on the status of "slaves" of Jesus Christ. Soon after, Bill received an overwhelming vision to begin Campus Crusade for Christ. Now it's a $300 million a year ministry. Yet the Brights receive a combined salary of $48,000. They don't own a house or car, yet they have impacted the world significantly. They have measured success not by worldly gain but by sacrifice in order to pursue God's vision.

[**Success is measured not by self-gratification but by sacrifice.**]

That same Kingdom Dream view of success is what we have longed for in our children rather than success defined by the American Dream. We have desired to raise our children to give rather than to get. We want them to have a ministry lifestyle in a shopping mall culture. Our hope has been that they would measure their success not by self-gratification but by sacrifice; not by grasping for more but by God's vision for giving their lives away. As Oswald Chambers put it:

> We are not called to be successful in accordance with ordinary standards, but in accordance with the corn of wheat falling into the ground and dying, becoming in that way what it never could be if it were to abide alone. [David McCasland, *He Shall Glorify Me*, quoted in *Abandoned to God*, Discovery House, 1993, p. 207]

We hope you have those same desires for your children because they are God's desires. Yet in the push and pull of everyday life, this dream can get fuzzy. How do we keep the Kingdom Dream clear?

World Changers—Vision or Control?

Growing up, my (Barry's) dad told me that in life 80 percent of the people don't know what's happening. They are floaters. Fifteen percent watch what happens. They are copiers. Only 5 percent make things happen. They are the world changers. He and my mom always encouraged me to live in that 5 percent—to envision how to change the world. Our children need to pursue that same approach to success. They must answer the question: "How can my life be used to change the world for God's glory?"

That question requires vision. But whose vision—theirs or ours? We cannot coerce our children to pursue our dreams. When children are younger, we can control their behavior—"Don't put your Legos in the toilet or I will take them away from you." We control their behavior by commands and punishment. Yet as they get older, that doesn't work. If we try it, it's called *control*. Trying to control them only leads to resistance and rebellion. Instead, we have to *influence* them. That

> **Our influence creates motivation to pursue God's vision.**

influence has the most impact in creating *motivation* to pursue God's vision.

To understand how to motivate our children properly, we must understand our own motives. Tim Smith, teen-parenting expert, says parents tend to focus on externals in their own lives: success at work, an active social calendar, and belonging to several clubs and groups. Those activities and duties often limit time with the family, and we can begin to view our children as objects instead of people. [Tim Smith, *Almost Cool*, Moody Press, 1997, p. 178]

Psychologist David Elkind adds:

> Parents under stress see their children as symbols because it is the least demanding way to deal with them. A student, a skater, a tennis player...are clear-cut symbols, easy guides for what to think, to see, and how to behave. Symbols thus free the parent from the energy-consuming task of knowing the child as a totality, a whole person. [David Elkind, *The Hurried Child*, Addison-Wesley, 1989, pp. 28-29]

Before proceeding, we must evaluate our motives. Do we want what God wants for our children, even if that is different from what we have envisioned for them? Are we willing to release them to pursue God's vision? Can we trust God even when they are not pursuing His vision? These are difficult, but necessary, questions that will determine how we relate to our children and how we influence them with the proper motivation.

In the connection between knowing our children and knowing God, vision occurs–both our vision for them and their vision for themselves. We must do all we can to expose them to as many positive *influences* as possible, but then understand that only the Lord will *motivate* them to pursue His *vision* for their lives.

So what is that vision?

Vision Defined

Vision is the ability to see what is not seen as already seen so it can be seen. Sound confusing? Think about an architect. He envisions a building that no one has ever designed or built before. He puts that design on paper. Then he builds the building. What he envisioned can now be seen by others. That's vision.

God has a vision for our children (and for us). He has a specific and unique destiny for each of us (see Action #7). Yet His vision is generally the same for all of us. What is it?

> God has a vision for our children.

TO SEE AND EXPRESS THE GLORY
OF GOD THROUGH OUR LIVES

For years this truth has been hidden like a secret in the Bible, but now it's bursting forth. Except for brief splashes of spiritual awakening, the church in North America has been largely anemic. We have built buildings and run programs while people in the world have been lost, sick, and dying. It's like blinders on our eyes that have kept us from seeing the power and glory of God. But now the blinders are being removed, and we can see His vision too. All of the writers of the Bible have seen the glory of God. For example:

- Moses and his leaders "went up and saw the God of Israel...they saw God, and they ate and drank" (Ex. 24:9-11). Then over three million Israelites saw "the glory of the Lord settled on Mount Sinai" (v. 16). After that the entire

Hebrew nation followed the cloud of glory by day and the fire of glory by night–for forty years!

- Isaiah ordered God's people:

> Arise, shine, for your light has come,
> and the glory of the Lord rises upon you.
> See, darkness covers the earth
> and thick darkness is over the peoples,
> but the Lord rises upon you
> and his glory appears over you.
> Nations will come to your light,
> and kings to the brightness of your dawn.
> (Isa. 60:1-3)

- Jesus granted us the privilege of enjoying His radiant splendor when He said, "I have given them the glory that you gave me, that they may be one as we are one" (John 17:22).
- The Apostle Paul proclaimed that "He called you to this through our gospel, that you might share in the glory of our Lord Jesus Christ" (2 Thes. 2:14). Paul amplified that "to [the saints] God has chosen to make known among the Gentiles the glorious riches of this mystery, which is *Christ in you*, the hope of glory" (Col. 1:27, italics added).

In the presence of His glory we can compare ourselves to no one else but Jesus. In that comparison we see how far short of the glory of God we are (Rom. 3:23). We understand why we desperately need the blood of Jesus to cleanse us from sin (1 John 1:7). We realize that no amount of personal attainment or success could ever make us like Jesus (2 Cor. 10:17-18). In the most profound way we grasp that only Christ can live like Christ. God's plan is not to improve us, but to remove us, so that the Lord Jesus Himself can actually live His life through us (Gal. 2:20). Our only hope of becoming like Him is that He lives in us (Rom. 8:29). [The ideas from this section were learned from Francis Frangipane, *The Days of His Presence,* Arrow Publications, 1995, pp. 16-22, 31]

This is the vision for all believers in this amazing time when the brightness of His glory is being revealed more and more in a dark world. How do we encourage our families to enter into it?

Unfolding the Vision

As wonderful as the vision of "expressing the glory of God" is, it doesn't come easily. Jesus worked with His disciples every day for three years before they fully embraced it. That should encourage us not only as we grow in our own ability to express His glory, but also as we build that vision into our children's lives. How did Jesus progressively develop the vision of God's glory in His disciples?

1. *Excite about the vision.* In a teachable moment Jesus gave His disciples a visual demonstration of His vision. Being fishermen, they could relate to fishing. He told His disciples to let down their nets to catch some fish. Peter protested that they had fished all night and hadn't caught a thing. Still Peter relented and put down the net. The result: They caught so many fish that their nets almost broke. Then Jesus cast the vision: "From now on you will catch men." Or as Matthew recorded it: "Follow me... and I will make you fishers of men" (Matt. 4:19). They became so excited about Jesus' vision that they left everything and followed Him.

Going with Keith Naylor, our youth pastor, Scott shared his faith with other students almost every week in junior high and high school. He saw many "fish caught"–lives changed through the power of Jesus. He bought into the vision to leave everything, follow Jesus, and fish for people.

We can look for ways daily to show our children the glory of Jesus and to sense His presence and power in and around them. God will give you ways to excite your children about His vision for their lives.

2. *Encourage with the vision.* Jesus gave His disciples the opportunity to watch Him "fish for men" by preaching, healing, and casting out demons. Then He gave them a shot at it. He gave them authority to do what He had been doing. And they did it. They preached, healed, and cast out demons (Luke 9:1-3, 6). What an encouragement to them to see the glory of God expressed through their lives!

Because sharing Christ is natural in our home, Jonathan, at thirteen, wanted to try it. The closest candidate was his five-year-old sister, Ginny. Unbeknownst to us, he went through a Gospel presentation and led her to Christ. When Ginny talks about her faith, she tells about her brother leading her to Christ.

Giving our children the opportunity to see "God at work" by witnessing, praying for healing, and standing against the Enemy will encourage them tremendously. Look for ways to involve them so they can see God's miraculous hand at work through them.

3. *Explain the cost of the vision.* Once the disciples caught the vision, Jesus communicated the cost. Peter had called Him the Christ. Then Jesus told the disciples that He must suffer, die, and rise again (Luke 9:21-22). That was enough to throw Peter off the edge. He took Jesus aside. "'Never, Lord!' he said. 'This shall never happen to you!'" (Matt. 16:22). Jesus rebuked him and told him he was of the Devil and didn't have God's vision in mind. Then Jesus made the application. He said if anyone wanted to follow him and fish for people, then he must:

- deny himself.
- take up his cross.
- follow me.

The only way to save life is to lose it. It's not worth it to gain the whole world and lose your own life (Matt. 16:24-28).

Jesus explained the cost quite clearly and often. It made some people mad. They turned back and no longer followed Him. Jesus asked the other disciples if they were going to leave too. Peter spoke for them: "Lord, to whom shall we go? You have the words of eternal life. We believe and know that you are the Holy One of God" (John 6:68-69).

In the sixth grade Jonathan started spending the night with some boys in his class. We got wind that some of these guys were smoking. We talked to Jonathan about it. He promised us that he wasn't involved. We talked about making a choice, not between right and wrong, but between his friends and Jesus. His relationship with Jesus caused him to count the cost, cut off the negative contacts, and continue to follow his Lord. Like the disciples, Jonathan had no place else to go.

Once our children see God's hand at work, like the disciples, they will never be satisfied with anything less. Yet the tension is counting the cost. Denying ourselves and taking up our crosses are not exactly standard fare in our consumer, self-centered society. It involves working with our children on daily choices to develop a lifestyle that counts the cost.

4. *Extinguish the vision.* Even though Peter made the great proclamation: "You are the Christ," later he denied Jesus. When a young girl challenged him and he refused to be identified with Jesus for the third time, it was the death of Peter's vision. The anguish only got worse as they nailed Jesus to the cross.

The process of developing real vision unfolds like this:

Vision ⟶ Success ⟶ Cost ⟶ Death ⟶ Rebirth ⟶ Reproduction

The death aspect doesn't seem very appealing until we grasp John 12:24: "I tell you the truth, unless a kernel of wheat falls to the ground and dies, it remains only a single seed. But if it dies, it produces many seeds."

The Cross Principle has eluded most American

Christians. Yet it is at the heart of successful, victorious Christian living and the key to vision. Carrying out the vision of "expressing God's glory in our lives" is so far beyond us that it is impossible. That's why dying is the only answer. God calls us to die to ourselves so that He can multiply His life through us. That's why we want to affirm Paul's marvelous statement in our families:

> I have been crucified with Christ and I no longer live, but Christ lives in me. The life I live in the body, I live by faith in the Son of God, who loved me and gave himself for me (Gal. 2:20).

When Scott almost died from pneumonia, he died to basketball as well. When Katie tore her ACL, she died to being the head cheerleader in her senior year. When Jonathan went through the humiliation of a difficult senior soccer season, he died to playing college soccer. Each experience was extremely difficult; yet God used those experiences to extinguish their vision for their lives and open the way for Him to accomplish His vision instead.

The less of ourselves there is, the more Christ can shine through us in all of His glory. And the earlier our children learn and experience that, the less painful dying to themselves will be for them.

5. *Execute the vision.* After the resurrection of Jesus, the disciples experienced resurrection as well. Once Jesus released His life into them through the filling of the Holy Spirit (Acts 2:4), they expressed the glory of God in everything they did. When people encountered the disciples and saw their courage, and when they "realized that they were unschooled, ordinary men, they were astonished and they took note that these men had been with Jesus" (Acts 4:13).

The Resurrection Principle raises up the vision, giving it

new life, multiplied power, and increased ability to express God's glory.

The reason Scott is a doctor today is because he almost died in the hospital when he was fifteen. Through that near-death experience God implanted in him an insatiable desire and calling to become a doctor.

When our children experience hurt, disappointment, and pain, we cringe. It hurts us when our children are hurt. Yet we can rejoice in the longer view that God will use every ounce of the hurt to multiply His ability to express His glory through our children.

6. *Extend the vision.* Through the disciples the Holy Spirit exploded the church around the world in a few brief years. Jesus had promised them, "But you will receive power when the Holy Spirit comes on you; and you will be my witnesses in Jerusalem, and in all Judea and Samaria, and to the ends of the earth" (Acts 1:8).

Expressing the glory of God through their lives, the disciples went out as witnesses totally abandoned to Jesus Christ. In a few short years the glory of God had gone throughout the world. The disciples caused a stir everywhere they went. In fact, the city officials in Thessalonica said, "These men who have caused trouble all over the world have now come here" (Acts 17:6).

God wants to do with our children what He did with the disciples. As they go, they will each carry an expression of the glory of God through their unique personalities that will further the Kingdom of God. God wants to use our children to express His glory both now and in the future, taking the message of Jesus around the world.

Looking back to Katie's encounter with the Brights shows us how all of these vision steps fit together. As we thought about how they prayed for Katie, it became clear that what God has taken Katie through over the last ten years illustrates beautifully not only the steps in her life journey but also the steps He takes our children through to fulfill His vision for their lives.

> God wants to use our children to express His glory by taking the message of Jesus around the world.

I remember that Vonette Bright prayed for Katie's future mate. Later that year we gave her a ruby ring for her birthday with Proverbs 31:10 inscribed on it: "A wife of noble character who can find? She is worth far more than rubies." We set out for her the vision of noble character through purity until marriage. (*Excite*) For a while she avoided boys all together. Her oft-repeated line was "All boys have cooties–of course except for you, Dad." But her junior year one guy caught her eye, and they dated for over a year. Could he be "the one"? (*Encourage*) One day at the beginning of her freshman year in college, she called home crying. She poured out her heart about how her boyfriend had broken up with her. We all cried together. This boy had broken her heart. And that broke ours. Her vision died. (*Explain and Extinguish*)

Remember Bart? He came to see her later the day she called us. They talked. Later Bart Garrett told her that he had begun to pray in the sixth grade that God would give him a wife who loved the Lord. His sophomore year in high school he began to pray that he would be the kind of husband who deserved that kind of wife. By the end of their sophomore year in college Bart knew that he had met the answer to his prayers in Katie. Katie knew that he was the fulfillment of her dreams. Last Christmas they were engaged. Bart had planned it for a year. When he gave her the 1910 antique engagement ring, he wrote her a letter, which he had framed. He ended the letter by saying, "I have loved you as a friend. I have loved you as a companion. I have loved you as a sweetheart. And I will love you as my wife...I will love you forever, 'til death do us part."

On June 20, 1998, Bart and Katie were married.

(*Execute*) As parents we couldn't have written the script more perfectly. God fulfilled this part of His vision for Katie and Bart. We anticipate that in the not too distant future they will have children. (*Extend*) Then He will fulfill the rest of the vision!

Modeling God's Glory

What will prepare our children to discover the vision of expressing the glory of God? We could find help in every verse in the Gospels. However, let's focus on four models that Jesus gave us and how we might apply these as a family, keeping in mind this comment from George Elliott: "Ideas, concepts and words are but poor ghosts until they become incarnate in a person."

Model #1. Compassion. Matthew 9:35-38. Jesus traveled through the cities and villages teaching, preaching, and healing. The crowds got to Him. They were harassed–beaten up and abused. They were helpless–hurled down on the ground and not able to get up. They were like sheep without a shepherd–without a purpose. When Jesus saw them, He had *compassion* for them. Jesus felt sorrow for the sufferings and troubles of those people. His heart broke for them. He wanted to help. What did He do and what did He tell us to do?

- *Let God break our hearts for people.* Pray with your children for God to give you compassion for every person you meet.
- *Learn to be skilled laborers going into God's field.* Before your family walks out the door in the morning, paint a picture of how God can use them at school, at work, and with their friends. Ask the Holy Spirit to give each one the right words and actions to meet the needs of others.
- *Pray with and for other laborers.* Ask God to surround your family with other believers who will be compassionate laborers, too. (Use the prayer strategy discussed

in Action #10.)

Each day around the breakfast table, create the time and opportunity to pray about and discuss how each member of your family can express compassion that day. Keep it brief and simple.

Model #2. Serving. John 13:1-17. Jesus wanted to show His disciples the full extent of His love. So He washed their feet. Back then roads were not paved, and people walked everywhere. During the dry times their feet were caked with dust. During the rainy season their sandals were covered in mud. Customarily the host provided a servant at the door to clean the feet of a guest, but in this case no one assumed that responsibility. None of the disciples volunteered. Instead, Jesus stepped forward in a room full of proud hearts and stinky feet. After He washed their feet, He told them that because He had washed their feet, He wanted them to wash each other's feet.

Building a servant attitude into our children's lives is intensely important. It will determine not only how they relate to others now but also what their attitudes and actions will be toward their mate, family, and other people later in life. People respond to those who lead by serving. What clues does Jesus give us on how we can serve others?

[**People respond to those who lead by serving.**]

• *Take action.* Jesus rose from the supper table, breaking away from an enjoyable meal, to serve. That's the hardest part: seeing the need, and then doing something about it. In our family it's easy for everyone to wait for someone else to serve. But someone needs to get up and take action. When we set the pace in serving, we can then invite our kids to do it with us. Start by getting up from the table and washing the dishes!

- *Move past the barriers.* Jesus laid aside His garments because they were getting in His way. He could have let them get in the way and then said He couldn't serve because of them, but He didn't use them as an excuse. We can help our children lay aside what keeps them from serving. Usually it is little things that become huge–a TV program, playing with a friend, or involvement in a game. If we lay aside what we are doing (reading the paper for example), then our children will follow suit.

- *Prepare to serve.* Most of the time we don't serve because we are not thinking about serving. Physically and mentally Jesus was always ready to serve, and that's why He grabbed the towel. Simply asking the question: "Who can we serve today?" will help prepare your family. At breakfast ask each person to pick one specific serving opportunity during the day. Ask them to decide right then so that they will have time to prepare for it.

- *Get into it enthusiastically.* Jesus poured the water and started washing. He didn't wait for anyone else to go first. What simple hints help our children get into serving with enthusiasm?

    —Do little things

    —Use common courtesy

    —Spend time with people

    —Think about what others need, not what we want them to have

    —Listen

    —Pray

    —Do something practical

Buy a special towel and designate it "the foot-washing towel." Pass it around after dinner, letting each one report on opportunities they had to serve others that day.

Model #3. Ministry. Luke 10:25-37. In answer to the question: "Who is my neighbor?" Jesus told this story about the

Good Samaritan. A man was going from Jerusalem to Jericho alone. He traveled a narrow, rocky road with hairpin turns that dropped 3,600 feet within twenty miles. Because thieves beat up and robbed people often on this remote and unprotected route, it earned the name "The Bloody Way." This victim had been stripped, beaten, and left for dead. Two religious types—a preacher and a musician—walked by, but they passed the man, leaving without helping him. Then a Samaritan, whom the Jews hated, came by. He had pity on the victim, bandaged his wounds, took him to an inn, and paid the bill. The "Who is my neighbor?" question wasn't that hard.

Read this story and discuss these ideas around the kitchen table, asking, "What can we do to 'get dirty for God' and help hurting people as the Samaritan did?"

- *Going.* The Samaritan was going along his way. "As he traveled," he met the need. We don't have to go out of our way to find hurting people. We see them every day. Who are they?
- *Loving.* He had compassion for the wounded man. The other two didn't have a high "compassion quotient." Yet the Samaritan overflowed with it. On a scale of 1 to 10, ask your family to rank their "compassion quotient."
- *Coming.* The Samaritan "went to him." He overlooked the risks and his own safety to get involved. Have your children think about the "safety factor" in helping other people.
- *Touching.* The Samaritan bound up the man's wounds, probably getting blood on his robe. Ask your kids if they are willing to put their arms around a hurting person.
- *Sacrificing.* When the Samaritan put this man on his donkey, it meant that he had to walk. He sacrificed to help this man. Ask you children what they are willing to give up to meet the needs of hurting friends.
- *Tending.* The Samaritan brought him to the inn and took

care of him. That was not in his original plan. He went out of the way, spent his time, and inconvenienced himself. Ask your kids to what degree they are willing to experience inconvenience to help their hurting friend.

- *Giving.* The Samaritan paid the bill, not just for the night but for two months. Ask your kids how much of their allowance they are willing to put into this project.

- *Continuing.* The Samaritan followed through by instructing the innkeeper to look after him, and when he returned, he would pay the rest of the bill. Ask your children if they are willing to keep investing in this person until this person gets back on his or her feet.

These are tough questions that demand answers. Like Linus in the "Peanuts" cartoon, who was plucking daisies and yelling into the wind "Does anybody up there (out there, down there) care?" people around us want to know: "Does anybody care?" Getting dirty for God will show our children in very tangible ways how to express God's glory.

Model #4. Witness. John 4:1-42. Hot, tired, and thirsty, Jesus stopped at the well. He asked a Samaritan woman for a drink. A classic conversation ensued that not only led this woman to believe in Jesus but many others from her town as well. How did Jesus talk to her in a way that communicated who He was? What can we teach our children from this passage that will encourage them to share their faith with their friends? To be as practical as possible, have them mention the name of one of their friends they would like to come to know Jesus.

- *Relax.* Jesus was tired and relaxed. Yet when we think about witnessing, we feel anything but relaxed. We can help our children talk about Jesus as naturally as they talk about a TV program. To create that opportunity, ask them to think of something fun to which they can invite an unbelieving friend.

- *Ask questions.* Jesus asked this woman who came to draw water, "Will you give me a drink?" What a great way to begin the conversation. Together write some questions they can ask a friend. These will help:

  —Do you ever think about spiritual things?
  —Rate your spiritual interest on a scale of 1 to 10.
  —Do you believe that Jesus loves you?
  —Do you love Jesus?
  —Do you mind if I share with you the most wonderful thing that has ever happened to me?
  —Do you know for sure that you are a follower of Christ, or are you still on the way?

- *Listen.* Jesus listened so intently to this woman that He heard not only what she was saying but also what she was not saying. Work with your kids on how to listen with sensitivity to what people convey beyond their words. Help them listen for needs, fears, problems, and questions. The better they understand their friend, the better opportunity they will have to lead that person to Christ. Role-play at the dinner table.
- *Establish a common interest.* Jesus told the woman of His thirst. Obviously she had come to the well for water. Jesus started the conversation about Himself based on common interest in water. Have your children list common interests they have with their friend that might open the door to talk about Christ.
- *Find the open nerve.* When Jesus told this woman that she had five husbands, he definitely hit a nerve. When we discover the open nerve in a friend's life, we get his or her full attention. Have your children think about what some open nerves their friends might have: parents, divorce, grades, and so on.
- *Avoid tangents.* In the course of the conversation this woman brought up social differences, water-drawing

instruments, her ancestors, and differences in worship. Nevertheless, Jesus kept coming back to this woman's need to know Him. Discuss with your kids their ideas on how to keep a conversation centered on Jesus.

- *Don't give up.* Jesus didn't stop when the conversation became a little tense, and yet He never forced the woman to listen against her will. Talk with your kids about how to take the conversation to the point of making a decision about Christ.

- *Be a creative conversationalist.* Jesus didn't memorize this conversation and repeat it with the next person He met. However, He did talk about who He was. Discuss with your children how to be creative with each person and yet still share the Gospel message.

Make plans for a sleepover, inviting a friend who needs Christ. Plan how to communicate the message of Christ.

Taking Action

Select one of the four ministry models based on which one you think will create vision in your family. Put the action steps of that model into practice.

Penetrating Questions

1. Which would you circle as the predominant emphasis of your family: American Dream/Kingdom Dream?

2. In what ways do you tend to control your children rather than influence them? What do you think God wants you to do about that?

3. How would you summarize/outline the Bible's view on God's vision of *expressing the glory of God through our lives?*

4. Can you say that you are totally abandoned to God's vision for your life? For your children?

5. How can you personally illustrate the six steps of developing God's vision?

6. What specific, practical plan will you design to focus your children on compassion, serving, ministry, and witnessing in *expressing God's glory through our lives?*

7. What one-sentence prayer will you pray daily asking God to accomplish His vision for your children's lives?

Fresh Ideas

- Invite people who are pursuing God's vision into your home. Ask them questions about what God is doing around them.

- Put as much effort into involving your children in ministering to others as you do in getting them to play sports or the piano. Have a family project to expose your children to a suffering world–feed the homeless, sponsor a child, visit a juvenile jail, host international students, or take a mission trip.

- Even if you have to change churches, involve your family in a body of believers where the worship is alive, the Bible is talked about warmly, people tell what Jesus is doing, and the youth program is geared to ministry, not entertainment. Support the church by driving, cooking, praying, or whatever is needed.

- Take your children to camps, conferences, and mission trips where they can deepen their understanding of God's vision for them.

- Pray for the Lord to bring along other adults who will take an interest in your children and support you in discipling them.

- Decide on a ministry activity that you can do with your children weekly.

- Take a training course in how to share your faith with your children, and then do it together.

Further Reading

Colson, Charles. *Kingdoms in Conflict*. Grand Rapids, Mich.: Zondervan, 1987.

Hybels, Bill. *Becoming a Contagious Christian*. Grand Rapids, Mich.: Zondervan, 1996.

St. Clair, Barry. *Getting Started*. Atlanta: Reach Out Youth Solutions, 1991. This booklet offers six weeks of follow-up for a new Christian.

St. Clair, Barry. *Giving Away Your Faith*. Atlanta: Reach Out Youth Solutions, 1991. This book trains students in how to share their faith.

St. Clair, Barry. *Influencing Your World*. Atlanta: Reach Out Youth Solutions, 1991. This book teaches students how to serve others at school.

St. Clair, Barry. *Taking Your Campus for Christ*. Atlanta: Reach Out Youth Solutions, 1993. This book teaches students how to radically love their friends and have a ministry on their campus.

Expand Their World

**How can we release our
children to change the world?**

"GET OUT OF THE HOUSE!"

Toys and raisins were strewn all over the kitchen. Three
kids from the neighborhood were hanging out. They had
smashed the raisins into the floor. Melted Popsicle puddles
covered the counter. Ear-splitting noises bounced off the
walls. Six-year-old Ginny and her friends hung on my legs. At
the breaking point, I shouted, "Ginny, get out of the house!"

That scenario has probably never happened in your
home! But if it has, you know kids can do more constructive
things outside. God feels that way in dealing with His children as well. We have been playing in the church and

> **God desires to use our children to fulfill the Great Commission.**

creating a mess far too long while God is telling us, "Get out of the house!"

As we move our children from dependence to independence, one of the greatest parental challenges is to prepare them for handling independence. For comfortable, suburban, American Christians that means encouraging them to pursue the American Dream–getting money, a house, a car, a boat, and then do it again. All the while we do the church thing. However, at the other end of the spectrum is God's Kingdom Dream: For our families to pursue His desire to fulfill the Great Commission–that is, "Get out of the house!"

Blessed to be a Blessing

As parents we tend to hold onto our children. We want to keep them close to us–even after they grow up. But for them to be truly independent, we must open our hand that clutches them tightly and say, "Get out of the house!" No doubt, God wants us to release them. He made that clear from the outset.

> The Lord had said to Abram, "Leave your country, your people and your father's household and go to the land I will show you. I will make you into a great nation and I will bless you; I will make your name great, and you will be a blessing. I will bless those who bless you…and all peoples on earth will be blessed through you." (Gen. 12:1-3)

Blessed to be a blessing! That is the message God had for Abram in Genesis. And He continues to shout out that message throughout the Bible.

Like any good book the Bible has an introduction, rising action, a climax, falling action, and a conclusion. In the introduction, Genesis 1–11, the drama is set up by describing God's nature, man's image, and sin's distortion. The rising action, Genesis 12–Malachi, explains redemption's story. The climax, Matthew–John, highlights Jesus' death on the cross and resurrection, the heart of which is summarized in John 3:16:

> For God so loved *the world* that he gave his one and only Son, that whoever believes in him shall not perish but have eternal life. (italics added)

The falling action includes the remainder of the New Testament, beginning with Acts 1:8, Christ's foretelling of Pentecost:

> But you will receive power when the Holy Spirit comes on you; and you will be my witnesses in Jerusalem, and in all Judea and Samaria, and *to the ends of the earth.* (italics added)

In the conclusion we get to visualize what God had in mind all along.

> After this I looked and there before me was a great multitude that no one could count, from *every nation, tribe, people and language,* standing before the throne and in front of the Lamb. (Rev. 7:9, italics added)

Clearly the message is that God blesses us so we can share that blessing with others in order that more and more people will be drawn to Him.

Discovering What God Is Doing

Throughout the centuries God has blessed people so they can be a blessing to others. That's His strategy to bring the nations to Him. Today His activity has accelerated even more. Caught up in the day-to-day activities of raising our children, it is easy to get isolated from God's worldwide activity, but He wants us to move beyond our little corner of Christendom and help our children discover the amazing things God is doing around the world. Look at these exciting examples:

• 28,000 people become believers every day in the People's Republic of China. In 1950, when China was closed to missionaries, there were one million believers. Today, conservative estimates say there are well over 60 million.

• 20,000 people become believers in Africa every day; that continent was 3 percent Christian in 1900 and is over 40 percent Christian today.

• In 1900, Korea had no Protestant church; it was deemed "impossible to penetrate." Today Korea is 30 percent Christian.

• More Muslims in Iran have come to Christ since 1980 than in the previous one thousand years. In 1980 there were 2,000 believers. After years of intensified persecution, there are now more than 15,000.

• 70,000 people become Christians every day in the world.

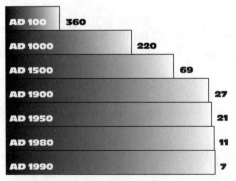

[Statistics from the Lausanne Statistical Task Force, quoted from Bill and Amy Stearns, *Catch the Vision 2000*, Bethany House, 1991, pp. 16-17]

Non-Christians per Believer

In A.D. 100 there were 360 non-Christians per true believer. Today the ratio is less than seven for every believer.

Let's go one step further—from knowing what God is doing to getting involved in it. Our personal conviction: God wants to use your children to finish the awesome task of completing the Great Commission!

With these statistics we can conclude that the Holy Spirit is working awesomely all around the world to bring people to Jesus. We are in the last phase of finishing the task. Just as the last quarter of a game takes the most concentration, completing the Great Commission must have intense "last quarter" effort. Involving our families in this is critical to God's plan. As hard as it is for us to release our children, we need to strongly encourage our kids to seize the amazing opportunity to join the mission on God's heart since the beginning of time. That means letting go rather than hanging on!

Because most of our children live in "their own little world," what can we do to help them cross barriers into other cultures, races, and socioeconomic levels with the love and message of Jesus Christ? How can our children learn and experience how to make a difference in "their own little world" and to expand their perspective until they have a passion for people around the world? These important practical directives will make the difference in our families.

God Is Already Working in Our Children

From a previous chapter we discovered the importance of helping our children from early childhood to realize that God is working—in the world and in them. Intuitively and concretely we want them to know the reality of Ephesians 3:20: "Now to him who is able to do immeasurably more than all we ask or imagine, according to his power that is at work within us."

From our earliest conversations we taught our children verses like Galatians 2:20, Philippians 4:13, and Colossians 1:27 to help them see that God is working in them. Indeed,

God wants to fulfill His destiny for them. To do that Christ must live in them and work through them.

Therefore, we want to bury this message deep into their hearts:

> GOD WANTS TO USE YOU BEYOND
> YOUR WILDEST IMAGINATION TO
> CHANGE YOUR GENERATION!

Involved in "See You at the Pole" from its beginning, I saw this principle in action. One sophomore in high school in Burleson, Texas, came up with the idea to gather around the school flagpole for prayer. He shared that with his youth group. They did it at their school. By the next year it had spread across Texas. The next year one million students participated nationally. At this time it has grown to more than three million students, the largest prayer meeting in history. One student allowed God to use him to impact his entire generation.

I told that story to my son, Jonathan, a junior in high school at the time. He decided to lead "See You at the Pole" at his school. It grew from twenty students to over 200 in two years. Inspired by a student in Texas, he realized that God could use him too.

In both of these teenagers' lives God used them beyond their wildest imagination. And He wants to use your children in some dynamic way as well.

What causes kids to view themselves as people God wants to use? In working with teenagers, I've noticed three issues that isolate children from what God wants them to do in their lives—often placed there by their parents.

Choices about "stuff." Jesus was right. We can't serve God and materialism. Yet parents in North America seem to think that they can have it both ways. That's why parents need to answer the question: How much is enough? Determine to live a modest lifestyle and have a plan to give away the rest. Children who have been given everything they want rarely follow Jesus wholeheartedly. It's really easier for a camel to go through the eye of a needle than for most rich teenagers to enter the Kingdom of God.

If your family does not have much money, then don't bemoan that fact around your children. For years our salary has come from people who give to our ministry. Every month we trust God for a paycheck. That has built faith in our family. Our children have watched God supply every need and never once fail us. As a bonus, our children have done everything they wanted to do–vacations, trips, and camps. Seeing the negative effect of money in many of their friends, our children are grateful they did not have much money. Be content with and thankful for what you have. Later on your kids will be grateful that they are not attached to "stuff."

As long as our children hold onto "things," they will never step out in faith to pursue Jesus' mission.

Leaving everything to follow Jesus. Denying ourselves, taking up our crosses, and losing our lives is not exactly the American way. But Jesus made these acts the measuring stick of discipleship (Luke 9:23). Anything that's placed ahead of God is an idol. Even positive opportunities become harmful to our children when they become idols: athletics, a boyfriend or girlfriend, money, popularity, grades, car, and the future. Harm comes when our children try to fill a void with these things or get them out of priority order. That's why Jesus said to seek Him above all else, then these will find their rightful place (Matt. 6:33).

A most difficult experience for my son Scott and me occurred in his sixth-grade year. The soccer team scheduled a game on Sunday. Our family honors the Sabbath day. For the first of many times we had a direct conflict. We talked it through. Scott didn't play. That hurt both of us, but it formed a conviction in his little heart that he has carried with him to this day: Following Jesus is worth giving up even the things most valued.

Spending time alone with God. Teenagers often ask me,

"Why get up in the morning to spend time with God?" The answer is simple: Unless you know Jesus "up close and personal," you will never have the motivation to communicate Him to others or to step across a barrier to make Him known in another culture.

Teaching our children by example to spend time alone with God will cause them to value it the rest of their lives. Recently we asked our children their most vivid memory growing up with us. Scott answered, "I remember walking out of my room every morning and seeing Dad in prayer or studying his Bible." When Scott was in the ninth grade, he heard a youth pastor friend at a Reach Out conference give the challenge to spend one hour a day with God for the next year. He took the challenge and still does that today.

For our children, that one discipline has proven to be the backbone of their walk with God. When our children meet with God every day, the Holy Spirit can speak to them showing them things that we as parents could never teach. They begin to understand and experience God working in them.

If our children can learn to choose against materialism in their early years by putting Jesus first and spending time getting to know Him daily, then the Holy Spirit will open the channels to show them how God can work in them mightily the rest of their lives!

Love Breaks through the Barriers

Because kids can act so cruel to the people around them, it can be quite an attitude adjustment for them to radically love others. One exercise I do with teenagers shows them how it feels *not* to be loved. They stand face-to-face with another person with one minute to make the other person feel like a jerk. Then they reverse roles. By the time they finish, the atmosphere within the room is depressing. Then they take one minute to show love to the other person. The place becomes filled with positive energy.

Sarcasm, snide remarks, cutting people down, picking,

and taking advantage seem the norm. One of the reasons Christ-filled people shine brightly: We have a radically different mode of operation. Modeling love to others creates quite an opportunity to impact our children.

The foundation for modeling love is found in 1 John 4:7-12. The beloved disciple gave us several key points that show us how unique that love is:

- Love comes from God (v. 7).
- The only way to love is to be born of God (born spiritually) (v. 7).
- If we do not love, we do not know God (v. 8).
- We know God loves us because He sent His Son as the sacrifice for our sins (vv. 9-10).
- Because God loves us, we ought to love each other (v. 11).
- When we love, then other people see God in us (v. 12).

Building on that foundation, we can demonstrate to our children how to love others–especially those different from them.

Let us offer three ways to help our children embrace their friends with God's love.

Experiencing God's love for themselves. The only way to love others with God's love is to experience it for ourselves–continually. Because of our selfishness, however, we get behind a "wall" that separates us from God's love.

> At this very moment Christ is standing behind our "walls." The walls between us and the Savior are primarily the work of our independent fallen natures. We have barricaded ourselves behind fears and carnal attitudes; we are held hostage by sin and worldly distractions. Yet these walls can be eliminated. [Francis Frangipane, *The Days of His Presence*, Arrow Publications, 1995, p. 140]

We need to constantly encourage our children and ourselves to eliminate the walls.

To shift the analogy, think of God's love as a shower. (I am a two-shower-a-day man myself.) Nothing refreshes me more than a good shower. But I can stand outside of it all day imagining it and nothing happens unless I get into the shower stall and turn on the shower. The water pours over me. I am cleansed and refreshed. In the same way we need to stand in the shower of God's love by getting into His presence and inviting His love to come over us, in us, and around us. We need that daily.

A simple prayer we can pray for ourselves and with our children is:

> *Lord Jesus, help me to step into the shower of Your love today. Pour Your love over me, into me, and around me. Cleanse me and refresh me.*

Praying with power for others. Family prayers can easily center only on our family concerns. That's not bad. But let's spread it out, teaching our children to pray for others' needs. Going one step further, we need to encourage our children to pray for their friends who need Jesus.

Our family did that during our children's kindergarten and elementary years. It resulted in some of their friends coming to know Jesus. When they got to high school, we helped our kids start a prayer group with their friends based on Matthew 18:18-20. Jesus promises that He will release all the resources in heaven on earth when we gather to pray–in groups of two and three. All through high school Katie had the names of her two friends–Stacy and Amy–taped on her mirror. She met with them every week to pray for her friends who needed Christ.

Out of that experience with my kids, I developed a national prayer initiative for teenagers called *An Awesome Way to Pray,* which teaches students how to pray for their friends. The heart of it:

Meeting
For

3

Christian Friends
times a week to pray
friends who need Christ

Many amazing answers to prayer have resulted from this. One interesting result is that it increases the "compassion quotient" in students for their friends. One girl wrote as a result of praying this way:

> Hi! My name is Becky....About two and a half weeks ago God started challenging me with this whole Love thing. So what is "loving your friends?" Loving your friends is loving God. I've noticed that a lot of my friendships are rather surfacey. This leaves me dissatisfied and wondering why. The truth is there's still some junk deep down there, junk that I want to be replaced with God's love. I know that I can never love God as much as He loves me, but I always want to make more room. [*An Awesome Way to Pray*] marks a turning point for me. It's a covenant that signifies love from God being *invested* in other people.

We can divide our own families into twos and threes and pray like this. With older children, encourage them to get with friends to pray. When they do it, God will use them to make a difference.

As a sophomore our Jonathan met with two other friends to pray. Within a few weeks seventeen guys were meeting at lunch to pray in threes. All year they prayed. Nothing dramatic happened. Then at the beginning of their junior year their class went on a retreat. Before a bonfire, the students confessed their sins to one another, repented, and prayed for one another. That lasted for four hours. God met those students there. From that retreat the junior class began to give spiritual leadership to their school. At the beginning of their senior year the seniors led chapel and at the end they washed the eighth-graders' feet! You know God is working when seniors even acknowledge that eighth graders exist. God used those seniors to change their school. At their graduation the power of that change was so evident that afterward parents commented that it was more like a worship service than a graduation. As a result the entire environment of this Christian school changed.

Serving people's needs. God's love actively meets the practical needs of people. Often Jesus met the immediate physical needs of people before He met their spiritual need. Jesus put a high priority on serving others. Meeting their needs provided evidence of His love.

> **Teaching our children to serve is one of our greatest challenges.**

To teach our children to serve as Jesus served is one of the greatest challenges for parents. As a couple we are still learning ourselves. For years this story has provided for us an illustration of what we are shooting for.

Baron Von Kamp lived in Prussia (Germany). A Christian and very wealthy, he used most of his wealth to give the poor jobs and to serve others in the name of Christ. Also he helped many students with their college education. One such person was Thomas, an atheist. Von Kamp opened his home to Thomas and paid for his education. When Thomas came home every evening, the Baron went to meet him so he could serve him in any way. He even helped him take off his boots. Thomas tried to argue with him and make him look foolish. One night in an outburst Thomas said, "Baron, how can you do all this? You see I do not care about you. How are you able to continue to be so kind to me and serve me like this?" The Baron replied, "My dear young friend, I have learned it from the Lord Jesus. I wish you would read through the gospel of John. Good night." That night Thomas trusted Christ. [George Muller, edited by Diana L. Matisko, *The Autobiography of George Muller*, Whitaker House, 1984, pp. 135-38]

Serving doesn't come in "five easy steps." It takes root when we allow the servant heart of Jesus demonstrated by Jesus washing the disciples' feet (John 13) to penetrate deep into our hearts, attitudes, and actions. We learn serving by practicing it. The following are some practical actions that can fuel a serving attitude in our kids:

- Share a ride to school.
- Offer to give up the front seat on that ride.
- Clean up the trays at lunch.
- Pick up books when someone drops them.
- Get the class assignment for someone who is sick.
- Give away something you like: CD, food, your little brother (!).
- Defend those others pick on.
- Include a lonely person in your circle of friends.
- Let others get in line in front of you.
- Speak positively when someone is being cut down.

Add your own serving actions to this list. Better yet, ask your children what they want to do to serve someone else. Decide two actions you will take this week.

Communicating the Gospel

We need a long-range plan to teach our children how to release the power of the Holy Spirit in their lives so they can boldly communicate Jesus Christ.

Truthfully, telling other people about Jesus Christ can be a fearful thing. John was a freshman football player. I was his hall counselor. I had become a Christian about a year before, and I wanted to talk to him about Jesus. I brought him into my room for that purpose, but I was so nervous that I started yelling at him. He started yelling back. Eventually he got mad and walked out of the room.

That must have been how nervous the disciples were when they were hiding out in the Upper Room before the Resurrection (John 20:19-22). They were very scared. There was no way they were going out of those locked doors and into the streets to talk about Jesus, whom they thought was dead. Fear is a dreadful thing.

Yet forty days later these same disciples were talking about Jesus to thousands with great confidence, boldness, and power. They went before the same court that condemned Jesus to death and told them, "You killed Jesus, but we're here to tell you that God raised Him from the dead" (see Acts 4:10). Courage is a wonderful thing.

What was the difference? They had experienced the Resurrected Christ and received the power of the Holy Spirit.

That is what we want for our children–not fear, but courage! God has called us all to be witnesses (Acts 1:8). So how do we help our children become a positive, dynamic witness? (We can hit only a few "hot spots" to work on. Get the books listed at the end of this chapter if you want to go further.)

Communicate love and acceptance to others. We never need to yell (like I did), embarrass, or offend other people. Out of a heart of love we must treat others with dignity and respect, knowing they are created in the image of God. Through Christ, God wants to restore each person to His image, and

He wants to use our families to communicate that message.

Relate Christ to personal needs. If our children are to learn to be sensitive to the needs of others, they need to have the conviction that Jesus is the only answer to their problems. Identify one need of one of your children's non-Christian friends. Brainstorm one practical way Jesus can help meet that need.

Talk from personal experience. Our children need to communicate their own personal experience with God. Our family began that process when our children came to Christ. We had them "write" their personal testimony. Our oldest son, Scott, wrote the following when he was seven:

Scott St. Clair

One day at the beach
My dad was sharing
to me about Jesus
crist and That day
I let Jesus come
into my heart,
June 13, 1980

Those testimonies are some of our most prized possessions. Those simple documents have kept our kids' initial experience with Jesus fresh all these years. As they got older, we worked with them to write out their testimony so they can present it to others. We have used the outline on page 238:

Communicate the message of the Gospel. Show your chil-

```
┌────────────────────────────────────────────┐
│  My Biggest Struggle:                        │
│                                              │
│                                              │
├──────────────────────┬───────────────────────┤
│ How I Met Jesus:     │ How Jesus changed     │
│                      │ me in my struggles:   │
│                      │                       │
│                      │                       │
│                      │                       │
└──────────────────────┴───────────────────────┘
```

dren the simple Gospel message. Help them learn the Bible
verses that go with it. Then take them with you when you
talk about Christ. In that conversation you can demonstrate
for them how to turn the conversation to Christ, how to
communicate the message clearly, how to ask discerning
questions, and how to challenge someone to accept Christ.

"Whoa," you say, "I don't know how to do that myself."
If you want to learn, then:

- Ask someone to teach you.
- Take a seminar on sharing your faith.
- Order these resources for you and your children: *Giving
  Away Your Faith, Taking Your Campus for Christ,* and
  Getting Started for follow-up. Order these through Reach
  Out or your local Christian bookstore.

One of life's great joys is to watch your children put this
process into action. For example, Jonathan joined a fraternity
his freshman year of college. He experienced some persecu-

tion for his Christian stance. Instead of backing off, he sent this e-mail to the pledge trainer, who had asked the pledges to submit one page about what was important in their lives. We quote in part:

Brother Vinson,

In order to give you a better insight on my life, it is imperative that I share with you about the three most important things in my life: family, friends, and faith (not in that order)...

(3) Finally, and most importantly, is my faith in Jesus Christ. I believe that all men are sinful and separated from God. Therefore, he cannot know and experience God's love and plan for his life. I believe that Jesus Christ is God's only provision for man's sin. Through Him man can know and experience God's love and plan. I believe that we must individually receive Jesus Christ as Savior and Lord; then we can know and experience God's love and plan for our lives. This personal, active relationship with Jesus is the only purpose for my existence. Therefore, my only purpose in life is to love God with all my heart, soul, and mind, and to love others as myself. Apart from Jesus Christ I am nothing. I believe that Jesus Christ lives in me. I believe that my sins are forgiven. I believe that I am a child of God. I believe that I have received eternal life with God in heaven. I believe that I can experience that abundant life right now.

These three most important facets of my life are my identity. Without them I am not.

—Jonathan Barry St. Clair

Not only did he send this message to the pledge trainer and other pledges, he sent a broadcast e-mail to everyone in the fraternity. It's that kind of conviction and passion that God will ignite in our kids' lives when we help them put these simple principles into practice.

On a Mission for God

To complete this subject we must see how we can involve our children in missions. All the other powerful actions are preparation to send them out. Jesus told us to be witnesses "in Jerusalem, and in all Judea and Samaria, and to the ends of the earth" (Acts 1:8). We begin with our family and friends; we move out to our neighborhood; then we expand to our schools and jobs; and then we go around the world.

At this point parents tend to freak out. Many parents of Christian young people do not want them to get involved beyond the youth group. Control or fear could drive that feeling. Many get bent out of shape about the "financial support" issue. ("I paid for a good education. I do not want you begging for money from our friends.") Yet God wants us to release our children, not reluctantly, but with great enthusiasm. Actively pray that God will touch their hearts and call them overseas.

> **Actively pray that God will touch your children's hearts and call them overseas.**

We have made it a point to design a mission trip for each one of our children and their friends when they were in high school. Do that! When you do, we have found that three benefits will result.

1. *A clear call.* God will begin to stir their hearts for the world. Scott and Cameron are preparing to go to Africa to determine whether they will practice medicine there as missionaries. That call has been a direct result of having taken Scott to South Africa when he was a senior in high school.

2. *An exciting adventure.* What you experience will not be dull. The summer we took Katie and her friends to Romania, we were stopped at the border. No one was getting through. The border guards had taken a couple of hours off to watch the Romania-Ireland soccer match. Cars lined up for miles, waiting. We prayed, and suddenly the bus driver turned the bus around on a one-lane road with steep banks on each side. He drove against the traffic with cars scattering everywhere. Then he headed this huge bus across a field. We reached a small road, which we traveled on for ten miles. Then we reached another border crossing and went through without a hitch. Kids were shouting and praising God for a direct answer to prayer–and one exciting bus ride! And that was just the first day!

3. *Amazing opportunities.* To stand on a street corner in Romania, watching our son talk to a Romanian teenager about Christ and lead him to Christ on the spot is one highlight of our lives. To sit in the audience while our daughter stood in front of a thousand people giving her testimony through an interpreter and then watching students come to Christ is one of our greatest thrills. If we take our kids "to the ends of the earth," God will give them amazing opportunities to experience His power at work.

If we, as parents, take seriously the challenge of this chapter, then our children will experience us lovingly leading them to Christ. They will watch us talk to our friends about Christ and loving a neighbor or coworker to Christ. As we experience the joy of missions, they will too. In it all, they will catch your passion to know Jesus and to make Him known.

God will build a fire in them to see "every people, tongue, tribe, and nation" come to Christ. That is God's blessing in our lives. At that point we will know that He has BLESSED US, AND OUR CHILDREN, TO BE A BLESSING!

Taking Action

Decide what you and your family need to do to "get out of the house." Work on a total family plan to love, pray, serve, share your faith, and go on a mission for God.

Penetrating Questions

1. How has God blessed you? What are you doing right now to be a blessing to others? (Be specific.)

2. How do you envision your children's future? How does what you envision differ from what you learned in this chapter about God's plan for their future?

3. In what ways do your children need to break out of "their own little world"?

4. What kind of choices does your child need to make about "stuff," idols, and spending time alone with God? How can you help them make decisions that will move them in the right direction?

5. What can you specifically do that will help your children experience God's love for themselves and help them pray for and serve others?

6. How can you model sharing your faith to your children? How can you involve them with you?

7. What are the options for taking your children on a mission trip in the next year?

Fresh Ideas

- With your family read Genesis 12:1-3, and then create a list of at least ten ways God has blessed you. Next, make a list of ten ways you are a blessing to others. Begin a "blessing book," recording in a journal how God has worked in your family.

- With your spouse, draw two pictures (no artistic skills needed). 1. Draw a picture of your expectations of your child's future. 2. Draw a picture of God's desires for your child's future. Be honest in discussing how they differ.

- Sit in your child's room for thirty minutes making a list of what is important to him or her. Which of those things are barriers to him or her in following Jesus? Which ones encourage him or her to follow Jesus?

- In conversation with your child, decide on the name of one friend who needs Jesus. Design a plan to show God's love, pray for, serve, and share the Gospel with that friend.

- Plan a night to write your testimonies as a family, and share them with one another.

- With your child, design a mission trip you will take together in the next year. Pray together for that country.

- Read aloud a missionary book to your family at the evening meal, before bed, traveling in the car, or on vacation. We recommend *Bruchko* by Bruce Olsen, *Through Gates of Splendor* by Elisabeth Elliot, or *Peace Child* by Don Richardson.

Further Reading

Elliot, Elisabeth. *Through Gates of Splendor*. Wheaton, Ill.: Tyndale House, 1956.

Johnstone, Patrick. *Operation World*. Grand Rapids, Mich.: Zondervan, 1993.

Olsen, Bruce. *Bruchko*. Lake Mary, Fla.: Creation House, 1989.

Richardson, Don. *Peace Child*. Ventura, Calif.: Regal Books, 1974.

St. Clair, Barry. *An Awesome Way to Pray*. Nashville: Lifeway Press, 1998.

St. Clair, Barry. *Giving Away Your Faith*. Atlanta: Reach Out Youth Solutions, 1991.

St. Clair, Barry. *Taking Your Campus for Christ*. Atlanta: Reach Out Youth Solutions, 1991.

Stearns, Bill and Amy. *Catch the Vision 2000*. Minneapolis: Bethany House, 1991.

Appendix

My dear friends:

The close circle of the St. Clair family has been broken-for the moment. On August 2 [1998], Carol passed into Glory. Now she is the picture of perfect health!

For the three weeks previous to her death, Carol prayed every night that the Lord would come to her in the night and heal her body or show her what His plan was. Each day she would tell me that the Lord had not answered her prayer. When I rolled over in bed at the sound of the phone on Sunday morning, I heard her voice. She said, "The Lord answered my prayer last night." Sleepily I said, "That's great. What did He show you?" "I had a dream. In my dream, I was standing on a porch. Jesus was standing below and He told me to jump. I jumped a long way and landed softly in His arms. Then He carried me up until I was consumed in the light." Then she asked me: "Do you think that means I am going to die?" "Honey, I don't know. But it's a beautiful dream." That afternoon her body collapsed and her heavenly dream became reality.

Carol's nine months of suffering are over. She handled it with courage, never complaining. No need for sadness about her. She lives eternally engulfed in the indescribable light of Jesus' presence. Right now she is enjoying all the wonders of heaven. But our hearts are broken. We have a gaping hole in our lives. Only God's presence can mend our hearts. Only His grace is sufficient to fill the hole. One day at a time we are asking for strength to make it through that day. Not surprisingly, He has faithfully honored His promises.

In addition to the Lord supernaturally lifting us up, one of the places we are finding strength is in the amazing influence of this woman we called wife and mother. For such a quiet, unassuming and selfless person, she made a large and indelible mark. On the one hand, I suppose we knew the power of her influence. On the other hand, her unassuming way caused us to overlook it. She became the living embodiment of the biblical adage: "Humble yourself before the Lord, and in due time He will exalt you."

Her imprint powerfully marked our family. You can feel her influence in the last letter she wrote to Jonathan:

> My dear, wonderful Jonathan,
> How disappointed I am not to be able to see you this weekend–to give you a big hug, snuggle, and talk. We definitely made the only decision we could, but I'm sorry it so affected you. I made it through the stomach test today (yeah-yuk!). The next three days the health care services will come here to the house (yeah) to give me IVs to boost my system to get me to Oregon. We all feel hopeful about that!
> I read 2 Timothy today in *The Living Bible*. Verses for me:
> **1:8** "For he will give you strength in suffering" (so many strength verses for me).
> **1:12** "For I know the one in whom I trust, and I am sure that he is able to safely guard all that I have been given…!"
> **Jeremiah 30:17** "For I will restore you to health and heal your wounds declares the Lord!" I'm claiming that!
> There's also so much in 2 Timothy 1 and 2 about young men like you, "chosen by God to be his missionary–to preach to the Gentiles and to teach them" (1:11).
> **1:14** "Guard well the splendid, God-

given ability you received as a gift from the Holy Spirit who lives within you!"

2:1-2 "O, my son, be strong with the strength Christ Jesus gives you. For you must teach others those things you and many others have heard me (Paul) speak of. Teach these great truths to trustworthy men who will, in turn, pass them on to others!"

I'm so grateful for all that you are learning—how you're being used and all that God has for the future! I love you, buddy! Mom

She indelibly imprinted her friends as well. Carol was the kind of friend that made each friend feel like she was their best friend, as evidenced by what one of her friends wrote.

Carol St. Clair was my best friend. And as I look around at so many women, I see that Carol was their best friend too. How can this be? Because Jesus was and is Carol's best friend and He was the One who gave Carol to us. In our needs and His timing and through her obedience, He came to us in her body for healing and nurturing, to love us and teach us about Him.

Her last week on earth reveals the power of that quiet influence. The emergency medical technician has called several times and written a seven-page letter to tell how she profoundly influenced him as they prayed on her last ride to the hospital. She went out of her way to make friends of every nurse who took care of her in the hospital.

I also saw how far that quiet influence extended in the week following her death. The cashier at the A&P saw Carol's obituary in the paper and called, asking for Mr. St. Clair. She wanted to tell me how upset all of the checkout ladies were to lose their favorite customer. Over 1,200 people came to the funeral home to say in one way or another that they had been touched by her sweet smile and loving concern. Over 2,000 came to honor her at her funeral. What's so amazing about that is those people were touched by her life without anyone else knowing that she did it–even the man who lived with her for twenty-eight years! Everyone who knew her agreed with what many said verbally and what many others expressed in writing: "She was beautiful inside and out." She lived that out right through the last day of her life. That Sunday morning I walked into her room, looked at her and said: "Honey, you look gorgeous." The full beauty of the Lord had already begun to express itself!

What Katie wrote for Carol's obituary characterizes her life: "A dedicated wife and mother, she gave her life away to others for the cause of Jesus Christ." One of the hundreds of precious letters I received came from a friend who summarized what those words meant to her:

> It was a privilege to attend Carol's memorial service. I have since acquired her obituary…it doesn't seem possible that an earthly life could be summed up in one paragraph, but it was.
>
> "She gave her life away to others for the cause of Jesus Christ."
>
> Maybe that one sentence says it all.
>
> For the past few days, I've been thinking that I would like to be more like Carol. I've since decided that I've got it all backwards; what my spirit really longs for is to be more like Jesus. Carol's obituary is now in my wallet. It will be a constant reminder to me of how God can manifest Himself in His people when they submit. With God's help, I will

strive to be a woman who gives her life away
to others for the cause of Jesus Christ.

What Isaiah wrote characterizes Carol's death:

The righteous perish, and no one ponders it in his heart; devout [people] are taken away, and no one understands that the righteous are taken away to be spared from evil. Those who walk uprightly enter into peace; they find rest as they lie in death (Isa. 57:1-2).

In life and in death we miss her more than we can express.

Thank you for your kindness and prayers on behalf of our family.

Jesus is still Lord,

Barry St. Clair and Family

*Reprinted from Reach Out Youth Solutions August 1998 newsletter.

Our Vision

To influence as many teenagers as possible to become followers of Jesus Christ.

Our Mission

To equip leaders for strategic youth ministry through the church around the world.

Our Resources

Student Life Skills

Life Happens...Get Ready—Helps students discover God's unique destiny in their life and prepare for the future.

The Moving Toward Maturity Series—A five-book progressive discipleship series that will move students to spiritual maturity in Christ. Each book contains five sessions.
Following Jesus
Spending Time Alone with God
Making Jesus Lord
Giving Away Your Faith
Influencing Your World

Moving Toward Maturity Leader's Guide
Taking Your Campus for Christ—Shows students how to reach their campus by radically loving their friends.

Help for Parents

Life Happens...Help Your Teenager Get Ready—Tools for assisting teenagers in discovering God's roadmap for their lives.

Reach Out Youth Solutions
3961 Holcomb Bridge Road, Suite 201
Norcross, GA 30092
Phone: 770/441-2247   **Fax:** 770/449-7544
Email: reach-out@reach-out.org   **Website:** www.reach-out.org